MW01138880

MARY, MOTHER OF APOSTLES

How to Live Marian Devotion to Proclaim Christ

By Giuseppe Forlai

Foreword by Marianne Lorraine Trouvé, FSP

BOOKS & MEDIA

Boston

Library of Congress Cataloging-in-Publication Data

Names: Forlai, Giuseppe, author.
Title: Mary, mother of Apostles : how to live Marian devotion to proclaim Christ / by Giuseppe Forlai.
Other titles: Madre degli Apostoli. English
Description: Boston, MA : Pauline Books & Media, 2018.
Identifiers: LCCN 2018002027| ISBN 9780819849748 (pbk.) | ISBN 081984974X (pbk.)
Subjects: LCSH: Mary, Blessed Virgin, Saint--Devotion to--History. | Jesus Christ. | Catholic Church--Doctrines.
Classification: LCC BT645 .F6713 2018 | DDC 232.91--dc23
LC record available at https://lccn.loc.gov/2018002027

Originally published in Italian as *Madre degli Apostoli* by Giuseppe Forlai © 2014 Edizioni San Paolo s.r.l., Piazza Soncino 5 - 20092 Cinisello Balsamo (Milano)—ITALIA, www.edizionisanpaolo.it.

Translated by Sr. Anne Flanagan, FSP

Cover design by Rosana Usselmann

Cover art: Palomino

The Scripture quotations contained herein are from the *New Revised Standard Version Bible: Catholic Edition,* copyright © 1989, 1993, Division of Christian Education of the National Council of the Churches of Christ in the United States of America. Used by permission. All rights reserved.

Excerpts from the English translation of the *Catechism of the Catholic Church* for use in the United States of America, copyright © 1994, United States Catholic Conference, Inc. — Libreria Editrice Vaticana. Used with permission.

Excerpts from papal and magisterium texts copyright © Libreria Editrice Vaticana. All rights reserved. Used with permission.

Excerpt from the English translation of *Collection of Masses of the Blessed Virgin Mary* © 1987, 1989, International Commission on English in the Liturgy Corporation (ICEL); excerpt from the English translation of *The Roman Missal* © 2010, ICEL. All rights reserved.

Texts contained in this work derived whole or in part from liturgical texts copyrighted by the International Commission on English in the Liturgy (ICEL) have been published here with the confirmation of the Committee on Divine Worship, United States Conference of Catholic Bishops. No other texts in this work have been formally reviewed or approved by the United States Conference of Catholic Bishops.

By Thomas Merton, from *New Seeds of Contemplation*, copyright ©1961 by The Abbey of Gethsemani, Inc . Reprinted by permission of New Directions Publishing Corp.

Excerpt from *No Man Is an Island* by Thomas Merton copyright © 1955 by The Abbey of Gethsemani and copyright © 1983 by The Trustees of the Merton Legacy Trust. Reprinted by permission of Houghton Mifflin Harcourt.

All rights reserved. No part of this book may be reproduced or transmitted in any form or by any means, electronic or mechanical, including photocopying, recording, or by any information storage and retrieval system, without permission in writing from the publisher.

"P" and PAULINE are registered trademarks of the Daughters of St. Paul.

Copyright © 2018, Daughters of St. Paul for the English translation

Published by Pauline Books & Media, 50 Saint Paul's Avenue, Boston, MA 02130-3491. www.pauline.org

Printed in the U.S.A.

Pauline Books & Media is the publishing house of the Daughters of St. Paul, an international congregation of women religious serving the Church with the communications media.

1 2 3 4 5 6 7 8 9   22 21 20 19 18

To the brothers of Our Lady of Mercy
on the 175th anniversary of their foundation.

———•———

"My little children, for whom I am again
in the pain of childbirth until Christ is formed in you" (Gal 4:19).

———•———

The task of the Virgin Mother is that of giving birth and gradually
forming Jesus in all those who must be "conformed to the image of
his Son" (Rom 8:29). Mary stands before us as Mother and teacher to
give us marvelous proof of how one becomes a true disciple of Christ
and to guide us to build our personality on the form of the Word.

Blessed James Alberione

Contents

Foreword

— • • • —

"Within your wounds hide me." That beautiful line from the prayer Soul of Christ has always fascinated me. Even in glory, Jesus Christ still bears the marks of his wounds, an eternal reminder of the suffering and weakness he endured out of love for us. In this book, Father Giuseppe Forlai says, *"Just as the risen Jesus willed to preserve in his glorious body the wounds of the nails, so Mary assumed into heaven body and soul, remains there with her perpetual compassionate sorrow"* (p. 21). That is why she is Mother of Mercy, a tender mother who understands our own wounds and sorrows. Forlai's insight amazed me. How can Mary's sorrows somehow still be alive? Isn't she perfectly happy in heaven? Yes, but that doesn't take away her compassionate heart, forged in her own earthly sufferings, especially on Calvary.

This book is full of such amazing insights. Forlai approaches Mary in a unique way that helps us understand not only who she is, but also how much she loves each one of us as her spiritual child, and how we are called to imitate her in bringing Jesus to the world. He draws ideas from the French school of spirituality, especially Saint Louis de Montfort; from Saint John Paul II, and from Blessed James Alberione, founder of the Pauline Family.

Forlai takes up an important idea from the French school, namely, that we relive the mysteries of Christ spiritually in our own lives. This relies on a sound theology based in Saint Thomas Aquinas, that the sacred humanity of Christ is the source of all grace for us. When we come into contact with Christ through faith and the sacraments, he imparts to us the grace he merited in each event of his life, from his birth to his death, resurrection, and ascension. In this book, Forlai develops the role of Mary, who was associated with Jesus in those mysteries. That is why she is so important for our spiritual life.

We see in Forlai's reflections a synthesis of great Marian saints. Saint John Paul II's deep Marian devotion sprang from his reading of *True Devotion* by de Montfort. His motto *Totus Tuus* expresses his total consecration to Mary. But John Paul II enriched this through his personalist approach to spirituality. He emphasized Mary's total gift of self, her spousal love as virgin, mother, and spouse.

Blessed James Alberione made a unique contribution by giving Marian devotion a strong apostolic dimension. He expressed this with the title "Queen of the Apostles" which is meant to spur us on to evangelization. Alberione saw the icon of Mary at Pentecost, praying with the Apostles as they waited for the Holy Spirit, as an image of the apostolic mysticism that Marian devotion can develop in us. As soon as the Holy Spirit came to them, the Apostles went out to preach the Word. Mary stayed behind the scenes, the gentle and hidden mother, yet she was the one who gave life to their preaching through her prayer. The more we make Mary a part of our life, the more effectively we too will be able to share with others the Good News about Jesus Christ.

Marianne Lorraine Trouvé, FSP
February 11, 2018
Feast of Our Lady of Lourdes

Introduction

— • • • —

Lyon, France, August 2013. With Father Philip, we went to the Sainte-Foy quarter of Lyon, near Fourvière, where the Marian sanctuary dominates the splendid city, an astounding nursery of saints. Coming to the piazza, we split up to be free to visit the building, each at our own pace and according to our own interests. After a quick walk around the sanctuary, I went to the seventeenth-century chapel of Our Lady of Fourvière. The statue of the Virgin with Child welcomed me, but I was surprised by how small it was. The statue was almost completely hidden by the white gown that encircled it, as if it were a child who had just received baptism. It greatly contrasted with the impressive majesty of the eighteenth-century basilica. The paradoxes are also reflected in the stone, which mirrors what dwells in the human heart.

After some minutes of prayer, I noticed dozens of memorial plaques on the sanctuary walls and nave. I drew near and, despite my ignorance of the French language, tried to understand the inscriptions. To my amazement, I discovered that many of these plaques commemorated the founders and foundresses of men's and women's religious congregations. They had begun their institutes in this holy place, or had often gone there to ask the Mother of the Lord for grace, light, and comfort in the many tribulations they would inevitably face as founders. I recalled that day in the Cenacle in the upper city of Jerusalem, where Mary prayed and interceded for the coming of the Spirit on the Apostles. In reality, that day has never ended in the life of the Church. Today, as then, the Mother of the Lord is present in every place where the Holy Spirit enkindles hearts and transforms limited and fearful people, even great public sinners, into apostles of the Kingdom. In my eyes the chapel of Fourvière had become like the Cenacle in Jerusalem. Here, too, the Spirit of the Risen One, through the presence of his servant, Mary, raised up new apostles—consecrated men and women dedicated to the missions, to the education of youth, to catechesis, to relieving the poor. I was enchanted at the thought of how contemporary our story is with that of Mary and the Apostles, as they lived in the days after Christ's resurrection.

Coming back to reality (but what is reality as opposed to the fleeting figure of this world?), Father Philip waited for me in the basilica's piazza. "Satisfied?" he asked. "Extremely!" I responded. But he didn't suspect the real reason for my satisfaction.

With this important and "unsettling" intuition, I returned to Rome, certain of having found the key to a problem. I could now unravel thoughts and desires, which, like a red thread, had been going through my mind and heart for about ten years in a disconnected way. Finally I understood the most important and urgent need for the Christian community: to enter into a covenant with Mary. She invoked the Spirit upon us so that we would commit ourselves to giving the Church new apostles of the Gospel. That was my light at the end of the tunnel. Finally we were there: Mary truly is the form of the Word, born from her flesh. And she is that form so intensely that, in our turn, to bring Christ to the world, we must enter the form of Mary.

This brief book intends to develop "the grace of Lyon"—the theological and spiritual idea enclosed, like a pearl in a treasure chest, in the Marian titles Queen of Apostles, Queen of Pentecost, and Our Lady of the Cenacle. All these titles send us back to the same mysterious and life-giving reality about Mary that was intuited and developed by the great French school of spirituality[1] three centuries ago and more recently in Italy, by Blessed James Alberione, founder of the Pauline Family. Unfortunately, these schools of thought are often merely seen as outdated or abstract ideas. I hope that those who read these pages will grasp that this teaching about Mary is extremely serious and beautiful. We must take a step forward in understanding and knowing the Mother of the Lord, above all in her role as the Spirit's collaborator in the

---

1. Founded by Cardinal Pierre de Bérulle (1575–1629), the French school taught the pursuit of holiness by emphasizing the person of Jesus, who lives his mysteries in us spiritually. It focused on the priesthood, adoration of the Blessed Sacrament, and devotion to the hearts of Jesus and Mary. Bérulle was a mystic, theologian, and statesman who helped bring about a great renewal in the Church in France. —*Ed.*

evangelical formation of all Christians, especially of priests and consecrated persons.

In the first chapter, I attempt to show the extraordinary reality of our being grafted in Christ by virtue of our Baptism. The Lord is the Living One who thinks, desires, and loves in the depths of every child of God. This adherence of our spirit with his is already prefigured in the events of his Mother's life. We could even say that Jesus lived and lives in Mary, since he was impressed in her from the very first moment of his virginal conception.

> *If God the Father willed to give the world the Redeemer through Mary, he will continue to do so until the end of time.*

In the second chapter, I reflect on Mary's presence and mission in the Church. Her presence starts from the Incarnation of the Word and culminates in the miracle of Pentecost. Then it continues in time, thanks to the Holy Spirit, who forms and builds the Christian community so that it might generate other believers as children of the Heavenly Father.

Finally, in the third chapter, I trace the profile of an apostle formed at the school of the Virgin Mary in the Holy Spirit. It is a school of evangelical smallness, privilege, and powerful intimacy with her Son, Jesus. If God the Father willed to give the world the Redeemer through Mary, he will continue to do so until the end of time. God does not change his style or method.

The end of each chapter contains a brief summary of the content, along with some texts for meditation from the teaching of the popes and the writings of Saint Louis Grignion de Montfort (1673–1716)[2] and Blessed James Alberione (1884–1971).[3] I hope this will be helpful to the reader. These pages call for deep reflection. Even if the language of the texts may sometimes sound dated, doubtless you will still be able to taste their beauty.

This brief work is more an appeal than a study, a starting point rather than a destination. It is a small contribution to outline the nature of the Christian apostle in the spirit of Mary. It is an "atmosphere" before being a book, with all the limits the reader certainly will find. Sometimes one can discover valuable objects even in ordinary and unattractive old boxes.

Dear reader, whoever you may be, I wish you the good will and discernment that will draw you, as Saint Louis de Montfort wished, to place yourself in the mold of Mary, the form of God. May Mary reproduce in you the features of the Divine Master, the unique and authentic Adorer and Missionary of the Father. If you think you cannot achieve this because you lack the strength or are too deeply marked by sin, throw your concerns on the Lord and confide in him. Let us together enroll in the school of Mary who has no greater glory than "to change great sinners into saints and apostles" (Blessed James Alberione).

---

2. An important member of the French school of spirituality, he founded the Company of Mary (priests), and the Daughters of Wisdom (sisters). Montfort emphasized total consecration to Mary. —*Ed.*

3. Italian priest and founder of the Pauline Family, Alberione emphasized the importance of the media for evangelization. —*Ed.*

Prayer to Mary, Queen of Apostles

It is truly right and just, our duty and our salvation,
always and everywhere to give you thanks,
Lord, holy Father, almighty and eternal God,
on this memorial of the Blessed Virgin Mary,
the first to proclaim Christ,
even before the Apostles.

Guided by the Holy Spirit,
she hastened to bring her Son to John,
that he might be sanctified and filled with joy.
It was the same Spirit
who made Peter and the other Apostles
fearless in preaching the Gospel to all nations,
with its saving message of life in Christ.

In our own day the Blessed Virgin
inspires by her example new preachers of the Gospel,
cherishes them with a mother's love,
and sustains them by her unceasing prayer,
so that they may bring the Good News of Christ the
Savior to all the world.[4]

---

4. *Collection of Masses of the Blessed Virgin Mary,* vol. 1, Mass of Mary, Queen of the Apostles (Collegeville, MN: Liturgical Press, 2012), 102.

CHAPTER ONE

Jesus Living in Mary

"Why do you look for the living among the dead?"
(Lk 24:5)

• • •

Jesus, the Living One

To say "Jesus is alive!" is not to state the obvious, thought it might seem so. He is alive not just in the sense of being a memory of some disciples or believers, or inspiring the ideas of some moralists, whether Catholic or secular. Jesus is alive in the sense that he is truly here now, while I write these lines and while someone reads them. Jesus is not only present but he is also contemporary with me, simultaneous with my action in the breath that allows me to live. He surrounds me and indwells me. He is in me, although outside of me, beyond my intelligence, as Saint

Augustine of Hippo wrote.[1] Jesus is seated at the center of my consciousness, but he cannot be captured. He is in the depths of my soul, not like water that stagnates, but like a fountain that springs up for eternal life (see Jn 4:14). All this is possible thanks to the gift of the Holy Spirit received at the moment of Baptism. Like a seed deposited in my soul, the life of the risen Christ can grow to full maturity until it occupies every corner of my mind, my will, and my affections.

This is not a fable or illusion. Certainly we can't be physically or psychologically aware of the presence of the Living One in us, but we can recognize it by its benefits. It's similar to the way I realize that I can see because light shows me objects. Similarly, I can understand that I possess the Spirit when I make acts of faith, hope, and love. Just as I do not lose my sight if I close my eyes or remain in the dark, the baptized do not lose Christ's seal in themselves because they are not aware of it or don't feel it interiorly.

This presence of the Living One does not violate our freedom. Only the devil possesses people's bodies without their permission, violating their liberty. On the contrary, as Saint Ignatius of Loyola wrote,[2] grace is always gentle, like a drop that falls on a sponge and is quietly absorbed. We have to try to make ourselves like sponges to absorb the sweet ointment of the Spirit, seeking to stay in contact with our inner truth and with the reality that surrounds us. We will see how this is possible through

1. See *Confessions,* VII, 10, 16.
2. See *Spiritual Exercises,* no. 335.

three points of meditation: Jesus, considered as the Living One; Jesus, who sacrificed himself for me; and, finally, Jesus, who wants to relive his mysteries in me.

Jesus Is the Wounded Living One

The life of Christ in me is an existence marked by *his* wounds, not only by mine. The Risen One is not an unblemished ghost, but a man whose transfigured flesh bears the nail marks from the cross—marks that shine like gems for his disciples (see Lk 24:39). The Risen One, who sits in glory at the right hand of the Father, is eternally the crucified. The Lamb who lives forever (see Rev 1:18) remains as if immolated, "as if it had been slaughtered" (Rev 5:6). The consequences of this truth for the spiritual life are immediately evident: Christ lives in me with his wounds! His wounds of love took the place of mine, which were caused by egoism. The stigmata of self-donation does not cancel out but transfigures human fragility. This is not poetry but pure Christian realism. Some "spiritual" persons spend their life in self-absorption. They make concessions to their fragility by excusing it as a mystical weakness, and they think that God closes his eye to everything. But that is not so. The Lord does not close his eyes. He opens them and looks upon us with mercy! And he desires that we stop gazing at our wounds and, instead, look at *his*, the only ones that save and that shine for eternal life. "Forget yourself" is the key. Whoever refuses to understand this truth will be blocked in their spiritual growth for a lifetime, exchanging awareness with a kind of egocentricity.

The wounded Living One wants to place his wounds over mine so that they might be absorbed by life (see 2 Cor 5:4). Therefore to *let Christ live in me* (see Gal 2:20) requires, on the one hand, that I free myself from the illusion of having to be "good" according to the spirit of the world. And on the other hand, it requires that I stop thinking that my troubled history or my falls are the center of the universe. Christ does not want me to be good in the world's sense, but merciful, even toward myself. I too shall one day be a risen one, just as the Lord is, but always wounded, a living one stricken but not killed (see 2 Cor 4:9). At the same time, however, this does not authorize the Christian to transform his or her weak or dark side into the focal point of their interior life. The center always remains the Crucified Risen One.

Jesus Is for Me

The Living One is the only one "who loved me and gave himself for me" (Gal 2:20). Writing to his disciple Timothy, Paul speaks of himself as one of the foremost sinners (see 1 Tim 1:15). He was not so much first in chronological order, but a prototype, a living example of someone who, in a radical way, needed the Father's mercy more than anyone else did. Here we touch a crucial point in the experience of grace. Only a person who is ready to recognize his or her own sin, and the almost infinite possibilities of doing evil, can be open to the reality of the *inhabitation*, the indwelling in him or herself of the Risen One who enters the Cenacle's closed doors and forgives every debt rather than condemns. One such experience is so important that—to use an absurd example—if one could present oneself before God without sin and laden with merits, that would still not suffice to be saved (see Lk 18:9–14). For this reason (developing the idea [of how sin affects us]), Blessed John Henry Newman wrote that "we would have to experience what sin is in the beyond if we haven't become aware of it now."[3] It is more important to open our eyes to what we are and to the malice that dwells in the mind than to focus on the account we will have to give for the faults we have committed. Then we will be able to make our own the cry of Saint Paul: "Wretched man that I am! Who will rescue me from this body of death?" (Rom 7:24). But those who gloss over sin and play games with God's forgiveness, while relying on their own pitiful virtue as if they could compensate, do not even know what sin is about. For them, mercy is no more than the omission of a local police officer who pretends not to see cars wrongly parked on the spots reserved for the handicapped.[4] But that is not God's mercy. On the contrary, by forgiving, God omits nothing; he creates. He doesn't look past us, but *within* us. In a real way, not a symbolic way, we can say that *Christ lives in the baptized in the form of his*

---

3. The author does not give a citation for this quote. We were unable to locate the source in Newman's works. —*Ed.*

4. "Some men are only virtuous enough to forget that they are sinners without being wretched enough to remember how much they need the mercy of God." Thomas Merton, *No Man Is an Island,* (New York: Houghton Mifflin Harcourt, 2008), 209.

mercy. He immolates himself continually for the baptized person in the temple of intimacy created in his image and likeness. The Lord is in me in the sense that he is eternally *for me*! In this way the blood of Christ is effective beyond time and descends upon the arid ground of our arid life, suffocated by the evil we do (or don't do, but wish to do with all our heart!).

Jesus Is in Me

The Risen One does not only want to be *for me,* he also desires me to be so united with him as to reproduce in my flesh his own human experiences and form one spirit with him: "But anyone united to the Lord becomes one spirit with him" (1 Cor 6:17). Fénelon wrote, "it is too little to consider it ["Christ lives in me"] with the mind like an object. It is necessary to have him within oneself as a principle. As long as he is only an object, he is as it were outside of us. When he is the principle then he's within us, and little by little he takes up all the space of our ego."[5]

That is not to say that the baptized lose their identity, but that everything that they are and live—joy and sorrow, hope and disappointment, fruitfulness and failure, death and life—can be divinized, Christified, and thus transformed into pure grace. Even life's darkest events, which would otherwise be incidents to reject, can become sources of grace and consolation. We only

5. Francois Fénelon, *L'Amore disarmato. Antologia dale Lettere* (Milan: Pauline Books, 1996), 173. Fénelon (1651–1715) was a French archbishop and theologian who wrote many works on spirituality.

need to accept that the Living One takes them from us and makes them his own.

This grafting of Christ's life into ourselves is possible thanks to the mystery of the incarnation: the eternal Word took mortal flesh in the womb of Mary. All that is divine has descended into the human, and all that is human has been poured into the divine and transformed. The contact between the reality of God and the reality of flesh did not create a dissonant note but a harmony, because the Father created everything looking at the Son, in view of him (see Col 1:15–20). Thus, due to Christ, all creation incessantly breathes the world of grace. For this, Christ does not put himself alongside a person's life, but by right penetrates that person to

A well-lived Christian existence is that of the baptized in whom Christ relives all of his mysteries.

his or her intimate depths: he is more *"us"* than we are ourselves! We need to have great love for the mystery of this "contact," which took place in the womb of the Virgin Mary. It is precisely this mystery that allows us to live all that happens to us in Christ. And this mystery allows the Word the freedom to incarnate himself continually in the baptized. The incarnation, however, does not happen only at the moment of Jesus' conception. The whole life of Jesus is a continual "incarnation" in the wandering ways of humanity. The Master of Nazareth is true

God and true man, and therefore all his earthly experiences are imbued with divinity. Living among us, the Son of God took on human existence. When he ascended to heaven after the resurrection, he brought humanity next to the Father forever. This truth has marvelous practical consequences. Since everything the Master lived is divinized, then the episodes or mysteries of his life, which we read about in the Gospel, have been "eternalized" because the divine never ends, it never sets, and it is never exhausted. The risen Jesus still incarnates himself, still gives himself in the Eucharist until the end of time, healing ills even today. He still speaks to us as to disciples—weeping, suffering, praying, loving without interruption. But this is possible because I freely offer myself to him, saying, "Lord I am sad, come yourself to live your sadness in me. I am consoled. Come in me to live your gratitude to the Father. I am dying, come to live your death in me," and so on. In other words, a well-lived Christian existence is that of the baptized in whom Christ relives all of his mysteries. It is not merely a matter of being good or bad, free or slaves, healthy or sick, famous or unknown, *but much more simply, everything depends on being one in him* (see Gal 3:28).

Naturally, the Holy Spirit works this marvelous exchange of life that makes us contemporaries of Jesus. It is not due to the individual's strength. This exchange occurs in such a way that the poor, earthly events of my life are changed into Jesus', and his eternal and glorious mysteries are exchanged with mine. We stand before a marvelous reality that makes us exclaim with Saint Paul, "It is no longer I who live, but it is Christ lives in me" (Gal 2:20).

Let us not believe, however, that this all happens instantly, or once and for all! Charles de Condren (1588–1641),[6] the first successor of Cardinal de Bérulle at the head of the Oratory of France, listed four steps to this gradual process of *Christification*. I offer this modern adaptation as follows:

1. *Adhesion.* I must fix my gaze on a mystery of the life of Jesus that best interprets the situation I am living. It could be a teaching or an episode in the Gospels.

2. *Appropriation.* Next, I can enter more deeply into Jesus' sentiments, desires, and actions as I understand them from the Scriptures. I make them mine, bonding my state of soul to his.

3. *Dying to the old self (annihilation).* If I appropriate the mystery in a true and heartfelt manner, my old self, interwoven with evil, must be unmasked and then die by "asphyxiation."

4. *Transformation.* The death of the old self leaves room for the new person created according to God, so that God's beloved Son might shine through.

---

6. Condren was an important member of the French school of spirituality, under whose leadership the French Oratory greatly expanded. Founded by Bérulle, the Oratory was an association of priests who lived in community for the sake of greater holiness. —*Ed.*

Jesus Living in His Mother

To adhere to the mysteries of Christ's life in order to be transformed in him is the goal and happiness of earthly existence. This path will be completed after death, in paradise. Only then in fact will we be fully "like him, for we will see him as he is" (1 Jn 3:2). While we are still here on earth we have to patiently bear the burden of the old self, who never dies definitively. To use a metaphor, we could imagine the self as a zombie in a horror film. When stricken, the zombie staggers a bit, but then straightens up and continues to run. In other words, as indicated above, between the appropriation and the transformation in Christ there is the stage of dying to the old self. We have to fight a lot to curb in ourselves the consequences of original sin, of our radical and profound inability to trust God. This lack of trust deceitfully sustains the old self, notwithstanding our declared good intentions. It makes the old self precisely one of the "living dead," someone terminally ill who never surrenders.

From the moment of her conception, the Mother of the Lord was preserved from the stain of original sin and its consequences in view of the merits of Christ. Mary always entrusted and abandoned herself into the hands of the God of Israel. Mary was never suspicious of God or of his fidelity to his promises, so she had no need of dying to the old self of which Paul speaks. In virtue of the Virgin's Immaculate Conception, every slightest contact with the mysteries of the Son's life transformed Mary into him. At every successive adhesion, by grace, she was transformed. *No creature adhered to the mystery of the Son like the*

Mother. No creature on earth was more Christified than Mary. The words of the Apostle apply to her more than anyone else: "It is no longer I who live, but it is Christ lives in me" (Gal 2:20).

This doesn't mean that Mary was sheltered from hard work. Even though she was exempt from original sin, her trust in God had to grow gradually deeper. Her trust grew as she closely followed the events in her Son's life in a crescendo of abandonment and silent adoration that reached its summit on the day of Calvary.[7] The effort of her Mother's heart is only partly like our own. While we have to die to ourselves to abandon ourselves to God, she only had to grow in the grace she already possessed.

To adhere to the mysteries of Christ's life in order to be transformed in him is the goal and happiness of earthly existence.

The transformation into Christ that Mary underwent has a unique aspect in the story of salvation because of the particular type of relationship that the incarnation sealed. The Virgin Mother formed the flesh of Christ in her womb, but this eternal Son, even before his conception, had formed a mother worthy of himself through a wholly unique

---

7. See no. 17 of Pope John Paul II's Encyclical *Mother of the Redeemer* for more on this theme.

and singular predestination in grace. We can assert that Mary is the "form of Christ," whom the Word himself had formed even before he began to dwell in her. Mary is the Mold of God prepared by God! This inter-relationship means that—even until the end of time—where Mary is, the Son will also be, and where the Son is, the Mother will also be. One who finds Jesus, finds Mary, and one who finds Mary, encounters none other than Jesus. In that sense, the comment in Matthew's Gospel about the magi's journey and arrival in Bethlehem is much more than a simple description of chronological facts, "On entering the house, they saw the child with Mary his mother; and they knelt down and paid him homage" (Mt 2:11).

To be set apart by the Holy Spirit in this marvelous and indissoluble union is no small thing. Here there are not two lives but one. In fact, Saint John Eudes (1601–1680)[8] used to speak of the Sacred Hearts not in the plural but in the singular—the Sacred Heart of Jesus and Mary. In human experience, a baby lives in the mother's womb for nine months, and after birth the child gradually grows and becomes autonomous to the point of no longer needing his or her mother. That was not the case for Jesus and Mary! As the Son grew, their lives were not separated; rather they became fused. The more the Master distanced himself geographically from Nazareth to accomplish his mission, the

---

8. Eudes founded the Congregation of Jesus and Mary to train priests and carry out parish missions, especially in rural areas. He was a prominent member of the French school of spirituality. —*Ed.*

more the life of the Mother was drawn out of her. Mary carried and nourished Jesus in her womb for nine months, and the Son, as he grew, began to carry the Mother in himself. Jesus made Mary the most perfect disciple by nourishing her with the word. Jesus thus "gave birth" to Mary! If we take the Living One seriously this will also happen to us. Little by little, as we offer the Master hospitality in our inmost being, we arrive, without even realizing it, at the point where we ourselves are the guests, nourished and hidden in God (see Col 3:3).

Jesus Is the Wounded Living One in Mary

The qualities with which Christ comes to live in the soul of a baptized person had first to be imprinted in Mary, the first dwelling of the Son and the prototype of every believer. The risen Jesus wants to live in us with his wounds, with his glorious weakness, as he willed to live in Mary. The living Christ in Mary is, above all, the Lamb who was slain. The suffering of love, witnessed to by the wounds the Risen One shows the disciples, must find its place in Mary, who shared with her Son the great tribulation of Calvary. If that were not true, then we could not say that Mary is most similar to the Master.

Let us then seek to better penetrate that sorrow, beginning with the experience of our ordinary Christian life. The baptized person knows, or should know, in a particular way, the sorrow of *compunction*, of *compassion*, and of *abandonment*. Compunction is the most beneficial sorrow in view of our salvation, and is certainly one of the greatest graces God can give us. We have compunction only when we finally realize that sin offends the Father, and is not so much a matter of concern over our reputation: As the prodigal son confesses, "Father, I have sinned against heaven and before you" (Lk 15:21). When we are faced with the gravity of our malice without excusing it, the only viable path is that of tears. The second sorrow we experience in life is compassion. Healthy, unselfish persons feel overcome by the senseless power of evil, even though they have not caused it, when they are before an injustice that wounds and afflicts the innocent. To perceive this sorrow of compassion is a sign of great intimacy with the humanity of Jesus.

Mary assumed into heaven body and soul remains there with her perpetual, compassionate sorrow.

Then we consider the sorrow of abandonment, which we experience almost spontaneously when someone or something very important to us is taken away. Mary lived the sorrow of abandonment and that of compassion, but she did not experience the suffering tied to compunction. She never turned away from the Father. But that doesn't mean her sorrow was less profound. In fact, who suffers more: the unmasked guilty person or the persecuted innocent person? Certainly the innocent person suffers more, because the guilty person at least knows that he or she caused their own sufferings!

Standing under the cross of Jesus, Mary was the only creature capable of sharing the frightening weight of suffering without fault. The beloved disciple could not, nor the good thief (the only one to profess the innocence of Jesus),[9] nor the leaders of the people, and much less the soldiers. At most they could have felt compunction, as did the centurion in Mark's Gospel (see Mk 15:39). Instead, the Mother who was so innocent allowed herself to be reduced to nothing in her very depths by the spectacle of a violent and wicked world that killed its own benefactor. She had the "privilege of compassion." In her heart are forever impressed the wounds caused by that bitter scene of incomprehensible and banal evil wrought by men who did not even know what they were doing and what they might gain from it (see Lk 23:34). Mary could experience the sorrow of the Son because the evil she witnessed did not blot out her desire for good. Only the one who despairs of the good will no longer cry about anything! Just as the risen Jesus willed to preserve the wounds of the nails in his glorious body, so *Mary assumed into heaven body and soul remains there with her perpetual, compassionate sorrow*. Because of this, Mary is the Mother of Mercy toward all of us. Here on earth we struggle and weary ourselves, though we may often fall, trying not to succumb to the weight of a senseless evil we may be unaware of.

---

9. "And we indeed have been condemned justly, for we are getting what we deserve for our deeds but this man has done nothing wrong" (Lk 23:41). Regrettably, these words are only rarely proclaimed during the liturgy.

Jesus Died for Mary

It would be a great offense to God's mercy if we didn't recognize that Mary also needed mercy. Some erroneously think that because the Virgin Mary was not touched by original sin, she didn't need to experience God's mercy! Her own canticle of praise shows this to be false: "His mercy is for those who fear him from generation to generation" (Lk 1:50). On the other hand, Christ could never have lived in Mary without having died for her. The life that I live, I live in the faith of the Son of God, thanks to the grace of recognizing that he gave his life for me (see Gal 2:20). This excludes no one.

Certainly we have to understand what we mean by the term "pardon," which we often have a limited idea of. For us to *pardon someone* means that we don't take account of the evil that has been done. Human pardon is often reduced, in a certain sense, to mere "forgetting," erasing a relationship, hoping to be able to begin again. If that is how we understand pardon, then Mary didn't need to experience it. The truth of the Scriptures, however, helps us to understand that when God pardons, it is not only a matter of forgetting an offense, but of canceling sin, eliminating it so his creature is made new and beautiful. Nothing has more to do with pardon than beauty! What does it mean to say that the merciful Father makes the person new? What does this newness consist of in terms of grace? In Scripture, "new" is the reemergence of the origin, it is resplendent. "New" is *everything that becomes again what the Lord had thought of and created*. When the Father pardons us, he brings us back to our origin, that is, to the truth of how we ought to have been. He is merciful above all because he makes all things new (see Rev 21:5). This pardon that restores us to the newness of our origins and takes us away from "old things" is the fruit of the Lord's death on the cross (see 2 Cor 5:15–17).

If we want to understand pardon correctly, in the light of Scripture, we could say that this certainly involves Mary too. The God of Israel used his creative mercy upon Mary, from the instant of her conception, creating something new and unheard of. She was caught up and washed in the blood of Christ before it was shed, so that in her the beauty of the original creature might shine forth. We shouldn't simply say that the Son of God also died on the cross for Mary, but that his cross was effective for his Mother even before he had been nailed to it!

Jesus Lives Completely in Mary

Jesus nourished himself on the body of Mary, and the Virgin Mother transmitted life to the body of her child: *the flesh of Christ, the flesh of Mary*![10] But that's not the most amazing thing. Rather, what should fill us with admiration is that through Mary's trustful abandonment to the word of the angel, the Virgin

---

10. "You give life to Jesus because he is your son. You receive life from Jesus because he is your God. Thus you are at the same time she who gives and she who receives life. You are she who gives life to Jesus, and from Jesus receives life." Pierre de Bérulle, *La grandezza di Gesù, Brani scelti* (Milan: San Paolo, Cinisello Balsamo, 1998), 100.

conceived the Word in her psychological and spiritual being. Christ lives in our hearts through faith (see Eph 3:17). Mary's faith, prefigured in Abraham's faith, transformed every aspect of her personality. It Christified her mind, the desires of her will, and the affections of her heart, making her Teacher, Queen, and Mother for us all. Let us look at what the Gospels say.

Mary's faith, prefigured in Abraham's faith, transformed every aspect of her personality.

Jesus lives in Mary's mind, in her thoughts, and in her mentality. The Gospel of Luke testifies to this several times saying that the Mother of Jesus pondered in her heart all that concerned her Son (see Lk 2:19). She meditated not only in the sense of thinking about the events or the Lord's words, but, above all, she let herself be struck by them. She received them even if she did not understand them completely. It was not that she elaborated upon what she heard or saw, but what reached her touched her deeply and worked on her interiorly. Mary did not approach the Son in a merely rational way, but let herself be formed by the events she lived. In other words, the Virgin Mary is *pure listening to a word that sparks thoughts capable of making the Lord loved with all the mind* (see Mk 12:30). But this is still not enough for Christification. Mary did not dwell in God in her thoughts alone, but she also possessed the mentality of the

Kingdom. She saw, interpreted, and evaluated the world as the Father and the Son do, not with purely human criteria. It isn't enough to cultivate divine thoughts in order to have a Christified mind. Above all it is necessary to have an evangelical mentality. This is where true wisdom lies. So who is the wise one? The person who sees the world with God's eyes and not simply thinks of him. Mary is the wise one par excellence. What is the Magnificat if not the song with which she recounts the heavenly Father's judgments as he looks upon the world of human beings? What are his criteria in making choices? Mary knows that God looks upon the poor. He confounds the wise of this world; he loves the humble and turns his gaze away from the proud. He fulfills his promises even when everything seems to deny them. The adherence of Mary's mind to that of Wisdom incarnate makes her the undisputed teacher of the evangelical mentality.

Jesus also lives in his Mother's desires, taking possession of her will. This grace is not only witnessed to by her words in response to the angel's announcement, but also by her behavior at Cana in Galilee. Mary is the servant of the Lord, who, precisely because she has experienced in her own flesh the power of self-entrustment, could say to the servants at the wedding feast: "do whatever he tells you" (Jn 2:5). Although she didn't know what her Son wanted to do, she let herself be led. Then she drew the servants into their own sense of entrustment. All this is truly noteworthy: Mary is not a simple intermediary who transmits an order (she didn't even know what it would be). She guides our interior life by pointing out the way of converting our desires to those of Jesus, the Master. She involves us in her abandonment.

Her adherence to the Master's desires transforms Mary into the "queen mother" of the wedding feast. She rules the interior house, which *each one of us is,* establishing it solidly on the rock of God's word that is heard (see Mt 7:24). Justly, then, we invoke Mary as Queen, not because she rules by power but because through her is manifested for the first time in the Gospels the total obedience owed to the Spouse of Israel, who inaugurates his Kingdom of justice and mercy.

Mary's adherence to the Master's desires transforms her into the "queen mother" of the wedding feast.

Mary reaches the apex of her Christification in her affections. Especially in this dimension, the Master of Nazareth drew Mary into his interior space from the beginning of his public life. After his baptism in the Jordan, Jesus began to gather his disciples. They were his new family. The ties of blood gave way to the love of an election founded on the hearing of the word by those who recognized they were poor in spirit. "Whoever loves father or mother more than me is not worthy of me" (Mt 10:37). At Capernaum Mary had to be involved in the change of affections that the Kingdom involved. The Son let her understand that the new belonging he wanted to establish was founded on different values. He said, "Whoever does the will of God is my brother and sister and mother" (Mk 3:35), implicitly inviting

Mary to free herself from the narrowness of the family clan. Mary has to empty herself so that her maternity (which is everything for her) is in a way suspended at Capernaum. Then Jesus seemed primarily concerned that Mary should again return to being a disciple. But let us note well that the goal of this return to the beginning of discipleship is simply to prepare Mary to once again become the Mother of the disciples under the cross.

This is the journey of the Virgin Mary's affections: to lose her maternal rights over her Son and to learn to take care of those whom Jesus loved to the point of sacrificing his life. Thus is accomplished the Christification of the heart, to love who and as the Master loves, leaving aside the preoccupation of having to choose when and whom to love!

Summary

The risen Jesus is alive and is our contemporary. The gift of our spiritual life is a fruit of Jesus' death on the cross and of his resurrection. Baptism grafts us into this mystery. Our old self has died with Jesus on Calvary. The new self is risen with him from the grave. The Lord ardently desires that we put our whole existence (thoughts, sentiments, actions) at the Holy Spirit's disposition. The Lord wants to relive in us his very life for the salvation of all. Thus, the gift of grace bursts forth from his life, continuing to pour itself out in time through every Christian.

This pathway of immersing our "I" into Christ happens gradually, without force. It means descending into the truth of ourselves accompanied by the Master's word. He helps us to understand and interpret everything that happens to us in the light of the various moments of his life as the perfect Man. With patience and fidelity, growing in love for the sacraments and personal prayer, we must acquire an evangelical mentality. This mentality bears fruit in concrete gestures and attitudes that emerge from the depths of our being.

The extraordinary model of adherence to the life of Jesus is his mother, Mary. The flesh of Christ was formed in her, and with her, throughout the hidden life at Nazareth, Jesus grew in wisdom (see Lk 2:52). Mary, together with Joseph, was the teacher of Jesus, the Master. She taught him how to live in the world, how to turn to the God of the forefathers of Israel with the psalms, how to await and reverence the Sabbath in the intimacy of family liturgy. Jesus' humility and meekness are the characteristics that best demonstrate the fruit he drew from the training he received from his parents.

God called Mary to be the mother of his Son. Her maternity was further matured in a different form of discipleship. From being Jesus' teacher, she became his disciple, even to the point of the most difficult lesson: the salvific power of suffering under the cross. The life of Mary grew, turning itself upside down! The mother and form of the Word let herself be regenerated and formed by Jesus, to whom she had given birth in an integral way—in the mind, will, and affections. In this way, after having formed her, the Spirit gave her to us as *Teacher* of the Gospel that converts the mind, as *Queen* in the desire to follow the footsteps of Christ, and as *Mother* in the order of affections, directed to feeling and suffering with and for the brethren.

Meditations

Christ is the supreme Teacher, the revealer and the one revealed. It is not just a question of learning what he taught but of *"learning him."* In this regard could we have any better teacher than Mary? From the divine standpoint, the Spirit is the interior teacher who leads us to the full truth of Christ (cf. Jn 14:26; 15:26; 16:13). But among creatures no one knows Christ better than Mary; no one can introduce us to a profound knowledge of his mystery better than his Mother.

The first of the "signs" worked by Jesus—the changing of water into wine at the marriage in Cana—clearly presents Mary in the guise of a teacher, as she urges the servants to do what Jesus commands (cf. Jn 2:5). We can imagine that she would have done likewise for the disciples after Jesus' ascension, when she joined them in awaiting the Holy Spirit, and supported them in their first mission. Contemplating the scenes of the Rosary in union with Mary is a means of learning from her to "read" Christ, to discover his secrets and to understand his message.

This school of Mary is all the more effective if we consider that she teaches by obtaining for us in abundance the gifts of the Holy Spirit, even as she offers us the incomparable example of her own "pilgrimage of faith" (see *Lumen Gentium,* 58). As we contemplate each mystery of her Son's life, she invites us to do as she did at the Annunciation: to ask humbly the questions which open us to the light, in order to end with the obedience of faith: "Behold I am the handmaid of the Lord; be it done to me according to your word" (Lk 1:38).

Saint John Paul II, Apostolic Letter
On the Most Holy Rosary (October 16, 2002), no. 14

Jesus Christ, our Savior, true God and true Man, ought to be the last end of all our other devotions, otherwise they are false and misleading. Jesus Christ is the *alpha* and the *omega,* the beginning and the end of all things. We do not labor, as the Apostle says, except to render every person perfect in Jesus Christ, because in him alone the whole fullness of the Divinity dwells, together with all the other fullness of graces, virtues, and perfections; because in him alone we have been blessed with all spiritual blessing. He is our only Master, who has to teach us; our only Lord, on whom we ought to depend; our only Head, to whom we must belong; our only Model, to whom we should conform ourselves; our only Physician, who can heal us; our only Shepherd, who can feed us; our only Way, who can lead us; our only Truth, who can make us grow; our only Life, who can animate us; and our only All in all things, who can suffice us. No other name has been given under heaven, except the name of Jesus, by which we can be saved. God has laid no other foundation of our salvation, our perfection, and our glory, except Jesus Christ. Every building that is not built upon that firm rock is founded upon shifting sand, and sooner or later will inevitably fall. Every one of the faithful who is not united to him, as a branch joined to the vine, will fall, wither, and be fit only to be cast into the fire. If we are in Jesus Christ and Jesus Christ is in us, we have no condemnation to fear. Neither the angels of heaven, nor people on earth, nor the devils of hell, nor any other creature can injure us because they cannot separate us from the love of God that is in Jesus Christ. By Jesus Christ, with Jesus Christ, and in Jesus Christ, we can do all things. We can render all honor and glory to the Father in the unity of the Holy Spirit. We can become perfect ourselves, and be to our neighbor a good fragrance of eternal life.

If, then, we establish a solid devotion to our Blessed Lady, it is only to more perfectly establish devotion to Jesus Christ, and to put forward an easy and secure means for finding Jesus Christ. If devotion to our Lady took us away from Jesus Christ, we would have to reject it as an illusion of the devil. But on the contrary, that is far from being the case. As I have already shown and will show more fully later, this devotion is necessary because it is the way to find Jesus Christ perfectly, to love him tenderly, and to serve him faithfully.

Saint Louis Grignion de Montfort,
True Devotion,[11] nn. 61–62.

Mary penetrated the secret mysteries of the Incarnation and Redemption. In the intimacy of thirty years of family life with Jesus, she grasped the whole spirit of the New Testament, which Jesus first reproduced in himself, in his holiness: "He began to do," while waiting for the hour when he would begin to teach. It was easy for Mary to pass from the instruction and school of the Old Testament to the instruction and school of the New Testament, in the school of her Son, the Teacher. What had already been taught, she now saw lived by Jesus. What had been foretold now became reality before her eyes.

The Annunciation was a great revelation. There is much to be learned from this event, and how many commentaries have been written! A profound treatise could be compiled from them. The same is true of Mary's visit to Saint Elizabeth, the Nativity, the presentation of Jesus in the Temple, and the

---

11. Saint Louis-Marie Grignion de Montfort, *A Treatise on the True Devotion to the Blessed Virgin*, trans. Frederick William Faber (London: Burns and Lambert, 1863) —*Ed.*

hidden life at Nazareth. In himself Jesus lived the life of the future Church, the highest perfection, heavenly communications.

Mary observed, remembered, and meditated. Saint Luke notes that after listening to the many wonderful things the shepherds said at the crib, "Mary treasured all these words and pondered them in her heart" (Lk 2:19). And again, after telling us of the finding of the Child Jesus in the Temple, Saint Luke writes that Mary "treasured all these things in her heart" (Lk 2:51).

Intimacy with Jesus

Father Joseph Patsch writes, "Having inherited the best qualities from his Immaculate Mother, Jesus greatly resembled Mary both in character and in physical appearance. Mother and Son reciprocally gave one another something of their own being. . . ."

Together with Jesus, Mary also grew spiritually. Her soul was enriched and strengthened in virtue. The heavenly Father looked upon her with joy and pleasure. Upon her too, he directed his gaze filled with blessings. The souls of Jesus and Mary felt united in the love of God.

A heavy veil conceals from us the hidden years that preceded Jesus' public life. In those years Jesus passed from youth to manhood, worked as a carpenter, and earned the respect of his fellow citizens. However, none of them ever imagined his true identity. "Among you stands one whom you do not know" (Jn 1:26). Only Mary and Joseph knew who he was, but they kept silent and waited for the time when God would be pleased to reveal the Savior openly.

Mary's Spiritual Growth

We will not attempt to lift the veil that covers these hidden years of Jesus' life, so full of mystery. We would not succeed in doing so. It is impossible to penetrate it. During those happy years, in the most perfect intimacy with her Son, Mary grew spiritually and attained the most sublime perfection. What Jesus would later say in his discourses must have been part of the Holy Family's conversations. In his Mother, Jesus found his first and most attentive pupil. If "from his fullness we have all received, grace upon grace" (Jn 1:16), and if Jesus "speaks the words of God" for all of us, and if the Holy Spirit is given "without measure" (Jn 3:34), so much more must Mary have been enriched by the fullness of grace. She stayed near the fountain and held in her hands the precious vase of her soul, ready to receive the water springing up to life everlasting.

Blessed James Alberione,
Mary, Disciple and Teacher[12]

---

12. *Mary, Disciple and Teacher*, in *Mary Queen of the Apostles* (Milan, Cinisello Balsamo: Edizioni San Paolo, 2008), 279–81.

CHAPTER TWO

Mary Living in the Church

*To each is given the manifestation of the Spirit
for the common good (1 Cor 12:7).*

— • • • —

The Spirit, Mary, and the Church

For the Church to draw near the person of Mary is not just an option but a duty. Both of these realities, Mary and the Church, were thought of, willed, and loved simultaneously by the Persons of the Trinity: Father, Son, and Holy Spirit. Within the space of this uncreated love, Mary and the Church rest as in a womb. The truth or reality of both the Church and Mary are not alongside but *within one another*. Let us seek to understand this in greater detail.

The *Father* loves the Son with a unique and exclusive love. The love of the Son is enough for him and he rests in it. But this love is not closed in a circle because it opens outward: creation, myself, everything exists as a result of the spreading of this love.

Everything that has life is connected to this desire of the Father to glorify the Son (see Col 1:15–20). The Father wills that as many creatures as possible might be united to this particular love toward the Only Begotten: he seeks true adorers (see Jn 4:23). In the mind of the Father, the Church is precisely this: the home of the adorers of the Son. It is not a benevolent association or a moral agency. In a certain way, therefore, from eternity in the thought of the Creator, the Church was predestined to exist even before she began her historic adventure on the day of Pentecost. The predestination of the Church involves Mary, a true daughter of the Chosen People, the first adorer of the new times, and therefore the first member of the community of believers. Mary *in* the Church is thus always in the Father's desire.

Mary is the first creature capable of entrusting herself to God, the Father of Jesus.

The *Son* receives the love of the Father and returns it in a uniquely perfect manner. As the incarnate Son of God, Jesus was the Man capable of returning the gift of the Father in a divine manner. As Bérulle taught, if before the incarnation there existed only a God to adore, with Jesus, an *adoring* God is born. He is thus given to us as a model of total entrustment to the Creator. To understand this mystery it is enough to contemplate the scene of Gethsemane: pursued by the leaders of the people led by Judas, the Lord touches the depths of anguish. He does not flee, he does not protest! He says, "My Father, if it is possible, let this cup pass from me; yet not what I want but what you want" (Mt 26:39). In similar situations none of us would be able to abandon ourselves to God if the Master hadn't taught us, and if we hadn't been clothed in his spirit of fortitude. Mary, too, was capable of this intrepid strength, for in the annunciation she was clothed with the "power of the Most High." Beneath the cross with the beloved disciple, Mary represents all those who spurn the fear of danger, dishonor, and humiliation. She does not flee like the others, she is simply *there.* Despite her sorrow, she had no fear of being dishonored. Before dying, Jesus entrusts his Mother to the disciple, and the disciple to his Mother, uniting in indissoluble matrimony the Woman and the Church.[1] Together they form the new family of God, which Jesus offers to the Father in thanksgiving for his everlasting love, resplendent even under the pall of apparent defeat on Good Friday. This act creates an amazing interconnection: The Church is at the same time *both* the community always thought of by the Father to glorify the Son, *and*

---

1. The beloved disciple represents the disciples of all time, so he can be seen as representing the Church. Mary, the Woman, is united to the Church, the bride of Christ (see Eph 5:21–33). —*Ed.*

the people gathered by Christ to bless the name of the Father with a faith capable of total entrustment. In this people that is the Church, Mary is the first creature capable of entrusting herself to God, the Father of Jesus: "Here am I, the servant of the Lord; let it be with me according to your word" (Lk 1:38).

The *Spirit* is truly "the Lord, the giver of life," as we profess in the Nicene Creed. The Spirit is the architect and the hand at work in the Christian community: he generates this community, giving himself continually to believers. The Spirit sustains it in life, arousing vocations and abilities (charisms), which are indispensable so that the Church might breathe and announce the Gospel. Without the Spirit there is no faith in Jesus, as Paul reminds us (see 1 Cor 12:3). Without the Spirit's presence in us we would not be able to taste the Fatherhood of God (see Gal 4:6). But above all, the Spirit "nurses" us *like a mother* through the sacraments, especially the Eucharist. The Spirit transforms bread and wine into the Body and Blood of Christ. We have to understand this reality well, because we easily fall into an overly simplified vision of the Spirit's role. It's not only that he makes the Church and nourishes it, *but the Spirit also manifests himself through it,* in a particular way through the saints, known and unknown, who are part of it.

The Holy Spirit finds in Mary a most pure crystal through which to diffuse his light.

Mary too, the first creature in the communion of the saints, is a "manifestation" of the Spirit.[2] This is so true that the Father's providence disposed that both the conception of the Son at Nazareth and the birth of the Church in the Cenacle should happen in Mary's presence. From the physical womb of Mary, Christ is born at Bethlehem; from the praying womb of the Mother, the Church is born at Jerusalem. All of this happens only through the work of the third person of the Trinity. Where the creator Spirit is, there is Mary. Where Mary is, the Spirit is also present, the one who forms Christians.[3]

The Spirit in Mary: Praise, Prophecy, Freedom

The Holy Spirit finds in Mary a most pure crystal through which to diffuse his light. In her, he takes all the space he desires. If we read Scripture, we cannot but admire how the woman at Nazareth was capable of the actions and attitudes proper to one who has received the outpouring of the Spirit. In particular, I refer to three attitudes that the Acts of the Apostles typically attributes to the baptized: praise, prophecy, and freedom.

---

2. In the sense that Mary was so attuned to the workings of the Spirit that everything she did reflected the Spirit's influence. —*Ed.*

3. In his mystic vision of the role of Mary, Saint Maximilian Kolbe (1894–1941) maintained that she was, in a certain way, a "quasi incarnation"* of the Holy Spirit. An impulsive but significant thought!

Kolbe of course did not mean that Mary was divine. He was trying to articulate her relationship to the Holy Spirit, in the sense of Mary being a "transparent icon" of the Spirit. —*Ed.*

The *praise* of Mary is a characteristic feature of Luke's infancy narrative. The canticle of the Magnificat sums up this foundational attitude, while referring us to a specific event. Mary not only praises but also lives in thanksgiving. Let us seek to more deeply understand this Marian feature, putting it in proper context. The person who magnifies the goodness and faithfulness of God before Elizabeth is a girl of about fifteen, involved in an extraordinary yet unsettling history. Mary is a fiancée *who finds herself pregnant by the action of the Spirit.* Only Joseph, a holy man , could find such a story credible. None of his fellow citizens in Nazareth would have been disposed to accept it. Perhaps Joseph—to silence the voices and guide his betrothed—in the face of the elders took upon himself the responsibility for this "fault."[4] Looking at things from a human perspective, the virginal conception raised more than one problem for the Galilean engaged couple. Yet—and this is Mary's admirable greatness—Luke records her canticle of praise and gratitude, not of lament or desperation. See what the Spirit does in her! He brings her to magnify an unpredictable and elusive God. Mary knows only that God keeps his promises, even when the darkness of mockery and the misunderstanding enters her life!

Mary's capacity to arouse *prophecy* is another aspect of how the Holy Spirit becomes transparent in her. We know from Scripture that the Spirit of God opens the mouths of believers so that they pronounce prophetic words (see Num 11:29). Such

---

4. See F. Manns, *Beata Colei che ha creduto. Maria, una donna ebrea* (Milan: Edizioni Terra Sancta, 2009), 35–39.

words reveal God's presence in history and interpret his designs. At the time of Jesus, the majority of Israelites bitterly thought that the Holy Spirit's action of among the faithful had been extinguished. There were no more prophets! It is surprising that at the visitation it is Mary—a young woman with no social or religious standing—who transmits to her elderly relative the Spirit who filled her. Elizabeth and her husband, Zechariah, represent the Chosen People, who had grown discouraged. It is Elizabeth who is clothed in the gift of prophecy in the act of embracing the Virgin. Elizabeth's tongue is loosed as she recognizes the presence of the Messiah: "And Elizabeth was filled with the Holy Spirit and exclaimed with a loud cry, 'Blessed are you among women, and blessed is the fruit of your womb. And why has this happened to me, that the mother of my Lord comes to me?'" (Lk 1:41–43). The Messiah and his Spirit are again in the midst of the people, not with the drama of a spectacular public manifestation, but in the humble person of the Woman of Nazareth.[5] Where Mary arrives, the prophetic vocation of Israel is reawakened.

---

5. Besides what I've said, I want to affirm that the most important feature of true devotion to Mary is the capacity for prophecy. Someone who really enters into intimate contact with the Virgin does not remain simply a spectator of the history or life of the Church, but becomes a deeply spiritual person, able to see reality with the eyes of God. A devotion to Mary that leaves things as they are, that does not get to real needs, would hardly be authentic! Where Mary is, there is prophecy, and where prophecy is, there is evangelical newness. Because of this, to make Marian devotion something merely routine or an empty tradition would be to falsify it.

Finally, it seems to me that we can recognize the action of the Spirit in Mary above all in her *freedom*. Saint Paul says, "where the Spirit of the Lord is, there is freedom" (2 Cor 3:17). In my view, this expression is valid for the entire Christian life! And I don't think I'm forcing Scripture if I affirm that Mary was the great model of evangelical freedom. She followed Jesus, abandoning everyone and everything. In particular, this is vividly illustrated by her presence alongside her Son during his Passion. Let us consider what the powerful persons who came into contact with the Master during his last Passover thought about him. Pilate had the impression that Jesus was a powerless man, perhaps mysteriously in contact with the divine, but certainly at the

> *We can recognize the action of the Spirit in Mary above all in her freedom.*

mercy of the blind hate of others. Herod Antipas tried in some way to convince Jesus to work a miracle to amuse the king's court. But Jesus did not deign to speak even a word to him. And in response, Herod treated him as a pitiful fool. Finally, the leaders of the people thought of him as someone who duped gullible people, and as someone possessed. Perhaps we don't often think of this, but to follow Jesus as totally as Mary did means to share his folly, his helplessness in the eyes of the world. In other words, it means to be an object of the same hate. It would require great detachment on our part to accept all this; it took even more for a woman of first-century Galilee. This is the freedom of the Spirit in Mary: the choice to bear the "opprobrium of Christ," his dishonor and humiliation, which touches every creature (see Heb 13:13).

The Crucified, the Spirit, and Mary

As noted, we don't find a Pentecost narrative in John's Gospel. Instead, the Church is born beneath the cross, from the spouse's open side from which blood and water come forth: the blood that redeems and the water that sanctifies. The blood is an image of the sacrifice of the Lamb, and the water, of the purification of the Jerusalem Temple. Blood and water descend mystically upon the woman and the chosen disciple, consecrating them as members of the community of the new covenant. The crowning of this scene occurs when the Master, "bowed his head and gave up his spirit" (Jn 19:30). Thus we have various actors in the drama on Calvary: the Crucified, Mary, the disciple, and the Spirit who seals the reality that is being signified. What is their role? What can we perceive behind the historic level of the narration?

Let us take a step back and recall the mystery of the *annunciation*. In the virginal conception there are three actors: the Spirit, the Son, and Mary. The Spirit descends upon Mary so that she might conceive the Word, and works in her so that the flesh of Christ is formed. The Spirit is fruitfulness and always generates life. Jesus, too, brings the Spirit who recreates: pouring himself out upon the sick whom he heals and the guilty whom he pardons (see Mk 7:34, Jn 20:22). Before dying, the Master once more gives the Spirit, thus creating a new situation and, even more, a new subject: the Church. I believe that we can consider the scene of the crucifixion in the fourth Gospel as a kind of *annunciation of the Church.* Just as at Nazareth Mary received the Spirit and conceived, so on Golgotha the woman mystically accepts within herself the chosen disciple, who is *another Christ* formed by the Spirit. After the death and resurrection of Jesus, the Mother continues to have only one Son: Christ, who lives again in the disciple transformed by the Holy Spirit.

Even today Mary looks at every member of the Church as if he or she were the Christ. As Origen (c. 185–254) wrote in his commentary on John's Gospel: "For if Mary, as those declare who with sound mind extol her, had no other son but Jesus, yet Jesus says to his mother, 'Woman, behold your son' (Jn 19:26) and not, 'Behold, you have this son also,' then in effect he said to her, 'Behold, this is Jesus to whom you gave birth.' Is it not the case that everyone who has reached perfection no longer lives himself, but Christ lives in him (Gal 2:20)? And if Christ lives in him, then it is said of him to Mary, Behold your son Christ."[6] The mystery of Mary, and also of the Spirit, is inseparable from the mystery of the Crucified and Risen One and from his fruitfulness.

---

6. Adapted from Origen, *Commentary on John*, Book1, ch. 6, in *The Ante-Nicene Fathers,* (Grand Rapids: Eerdmans, 1978), 300.

Mary in the Church

On Calvary Jesus offered his Mother to the beloved disciple: "here is your mother" (Jn 19:27). At that moment, this was the final and the only reality he could give. It is always like that, the most precious things are given at the end! The offering of Jesus' body and his gift of Mary are simultaneous. We have much to reflect on in this regard, much to contemplate in silence. Often we take for granted the Lord's action here, his last testament, and consider this as something devotional. In reality, we ought to stop and fully weigh this event's meaning, beginning with the consideration that Jesus did not entrust the disciple—and with him whoever would follow him carrying his or her own cross—to the most notable among them, or to an important member of the Temple (for example, Nicodemus). Rather, Jesus entrusts John to a poor widow, who counts for nothing in the eyes of the religious leaders of the time. When we justly address Mary with the title "queen," we have to remind ourselves that her queenship is an aspect of the royal status of her crucified Son. To accept the "reign" of Mary means to accept the same logic that made Paul cry out: "Whenever I am weak, then I am strong" (2 Cor 12:10). This is not triumphalistic but humble!

Since the gift of Mary, a woman *living* in the Spirit (and so truly present in the Church) comes from the weaving of times past that reach effectively into the present, let us seek to understand better the depth of the Lord's entrustment. Let us ask ourselves: What does it mean concretely to "take into one's own

house" (or "among one's own things")[7] the Mother of Jesus?
What change of perspective does this give us? What conversion?
I deliberately use the term "conversion" because that is what it
requires. Let us seek to specify, to deepen the titles that Blessed
James Alberione loved to emphasize in explaining our relationship with Mary: *Teacher, Queen*, and *Mother*. To this I want to
add some thoughts on the memory of Mary in the Church, and
on her ministry of consolation toward sinners and the afflicted.

Mary, Teacher in the Church

To take Mary into one's interior dwelling means, above all, to
go to her school. She teaches us a Gospel lesson of fundamental
importance through her very way of being "mother." Mary was
mother *virginally*! Her motherhood—not through the interven-
tion of man but through the incarnation of the Son of God—was
quickly applied to the Church. The Church is "mother" of the
brothers and sisters of Christ by the action of the Holy Spirit at
the baptismal font.

In what specific way is the Church "virgin"? She is virgin in
the sense that she generates persons to the faith not through fas-
cinating or fashionable human words, but thanks to the foolish
preaching of the cross (see 1 Cor 1:17–25). Mary's virginity
reminds us that it was impossible for the coming of the Word to
depend on human merits. Similarly the *virginity of the Church*

---

7. This is the literal translation of the Greek text of John. —*Ed.*

reminds us that it is impossible for the Church to bring forth new Christians through her own human efforts. New members do not depend on the availability of substantial means, and much less on power and privilege. From this truth comes the maxim: *the renunciation of worldly power is the virginity of the Church.* Mary is thus a teacher who, by her very existence and not with words, teaches that in the Church's life everything is primarily a gift of mercy. It is a difficult lesson to accept because her virginal maternity has no exceptions. The Christian community is fruitful with new children *only* to the extent that

To take Mary into one's interior dwelling means, above all, to go to her school.

it depends on the grace of God and entrusts itself to this in poverty of spirit. We become authentic evangelizers if we say our "yes" to the Word as Mary did, renouncing the persuasive power of purely human means of promotion. To adopt a worldly mentality in proclaiming the Gospel of Jesus is profoundly "anti-Marian." The power of the Most High descends upon the Virgin when she says, "I know not man." She doesn't say, "you will see what I can do." We might reject this profound teaching that the Mother of the Lord offers us. We might think it's outdated or idealistic! But the results of a *non-virginal* logic are very costly. Perhaps we will conceive affiliates, but not sons and daughters. We will gain aggregates, but not brothers and sisters!

Mary, Queen in the Communion of Saints

In the fifth glorious mystery of the Rosary, we contemplate Mary crowned Queen of Angels and Saints. For people today, "royalty" is something that survives only in tabloids. The word "king" originally meant one who rules, guides, and forges ahead to mark out the path. In that sense God the Father rules history, that is, guides it to a good end, even when we see things falling apart and only ruins around us. What does it mean to say that Mary is "queen" among the saints? It means that she guides the Church toward its Lord. Or better, it means that the community of the baptized remains the "Church of Christ" only if it is ruled by a *Marian mode* of existence. This exemplary model hinges on two things: the faith of Mary, and Mary's way of loving.

The faith of the Virgin Mary took the word of God seriously. We must not discount that fact. Many Christians today read the Bible, ponder it, and pray with it. Although this is always to be desired, this is not enough. Mary took the word seriously because she chose to live under its power; she chose to hang on God's every word. If we were to imagine Mary's attitude in heaven, we might imagine her with her ear glued, as it were, to the lips of her Son, ready to receive his slightest whisper. Life's events and needs did not control her, but history read in the light of God's word and promises. Mary listened to these far from the noise of merely human thoughts about God. If Mary had paid attention to the ideas that she had about the God of Israel before the annunciation, she would not have become the Mother of the Word!

In the second place, the Church assumes a Marian style when she loves as the Woman of Nazareth loved. Certainly, we could say that Mary loved her Son because she had conceived him, given birth to him, raised him, and followed him. The Mother gave the Redeemer to humanity by saying her "yes." In that gesture of incalculable greatness, she gave herself freely to the Father. But this is not the love that makes Mary a model for the Church.

Where would we have to look? To what mystery of her existence? To that of the cross. There, as the mystic Adrienne von Speyr intuited magnificently, Mary no longer gives the Son to the world. Instead, he gives her to the Church in the person of the disciple.[8] In this we find the greatest example of Mary's love. When she no longer had anything to give, she allowed herself to be given by God

The faith of the Virgin Mary took the word of God seriously.

to another. This is an incredibly profound mystery. This is love tested to its limit *because it is precisely when we no longer have anything to give that it becomes possible for us to make a gift of ourselves, accepting in peace the truth of our own personal poverty.* Here Mary's queenship reaches its apex. She rules and guides us

---

8. See Adrienne von Speyr, *Handmaid of the Lord* (San Francisco: Ignatius Press, 1985), 145.

along the way of that love—a radically authentic way because she has nothing *of her own* to give at that moment except her poverty.

Mary, Mother of the Disciples

At the end of her earthly life, the Mother of Jesus was assumed into heaven body and soul. This marvel of grace is aimed not only at fullness of life in the risen Son, but also at perpetuating the mission proper to Mary. That mission is to collaborate in the birth and growth of Christ in believers. We may ask ourselves: How does the Virgin continue to exercise this mystical maternity? Let us return to Scripture. The Virgin in the Cenacle invokes the descent of the Spirit who will transform the fearful and silent disciples into apostles capable of going to the ends of the earth to announce the Gospel and to face martyrdom (see Acts 2).

Mary is our *spiritual mother* because she continues this ministry of invoking the Spirit for the Lord's brothers and sisters on earth. The image through which we can express this mystery is certainly inadequate, but can be evocative: she whom the Spirit of the Risen One filled effectively and definitively asks the One who inhabits her to also grasp us and transform us in the Son, the Apostle of the Father. In other words, the plea of the Paraclete who cries within us, "Abba! Father!" (Rom 8:15), is heard by Mary through a kind of co-naturality, for she is the first creature transformed by the Spirit. And by her this plea is translated into a pure invocation before the throne of God on our behalf, so that the Spirit of adoptive sons and daughters continues to reach and console us. Such is the virtuous cycle of this *epiclesis* (calling down of the Spirit) that unites the Mother to the brothers and sisters of the Son.

Thus, Mary's maternity toward us is not simply a metaphor. It is strictly tied to the mystery of the *continual invocation of the Spirit,* without which neither the Church nor the Christian life could exist. Together with the saints in that eternal cenacle, which is paradise, Mary prays incessantly for us. The Mother teaches each Christian that there is no eternal life without dependence on the life of the Spirit, there is no Church without charisms, and there is no communion among us without a heartfelt and continual plea to be led by the hand toward the fullness of truth that the Spirit bestows (see Jn 16:13).

Mary, Memory of the Church

Mary's intercession in the Cenacle continued in her presence as a simple believer in the primitive community of Jerusalem. She too shared the daily bread with the baptized and broke the Eucharistic bread with the disciples. It is very important to keep in mind Mary's daily manner of living in the midst of others, in a hidden way, without particular roles that conferred authority on her. Yet even if she did not have official recognition or any signs of such recognition, her presence made a difference and clearly pointed out her service, that of *memory*. During the earthly life of Jesus, his Mother carried everything in her heart. She reflected on it; she compared the words of the angel to what was gradually unfolding before her eyes. She often pondered, mostly she adored in silence, always she guarded mysteries that were greater than her and all of us. In that early community Mary carried out the role of being the *guardian of the memory of the Son*. As long as she was there, no one could say that Christ was an imaginative divine character or only apparently a human.[9]

Mary carried out the role of being the guardian of the memory of the Son.

No, the Lord is real, incarnate. It is impossible to manipulate Mary's memory to one's own advantage. She did not "think it up" or "dream it"; she touched him, cared for him, nurtured him, observed his growth and his becoming man. She remembers what happened from the beginning and she knows, better than the apostles, that the true Life was made visible (see 1 Jn 1:1–2), that he moved in her womb. Finally at the cross she saw his agony and death—for his people. In the

---

9. In the creed that we pray and profess in the Sunday liturgy, another historical personality witnesses to the reality of Christ's flesh: Pilate, *under whom Jesus suffered*. But the difference is that the Roman procurator was an involuntary witness, while Mary chose to be one. Pilate left his encounter with the Master frightened and perplexed, but Mary, definitively saved. Pilate chose compromise to avoid inciting the leaders of the people, but Mary espoused a radical following of Christ without fear of loss.

community of Jerusalem, Mary was witness to the flesh of Christ, to the experiential reality that, with its power, heals and restores all it encounters (see Lk 6:19).

While in the community of Jerusalem the Mother of the Lord didn't perform any "ecclesiastical" function, her assigned task was even greater. She was the minister of the memory of the incarnation and passion of her Son, of that blessed flesh that grew and suffered under her eyes. Perhaps the beloved disciple's gesture in taking Mary into his own house symbolizes the need for the baptized to take charge of that same *memory of the flesh.* That memory makes Christianity not a philosophy but a way of life. It involves the exciting yet challenging reality of following Jesus. In the end Mary tells us just this: one loves the Lord in the whole reality of his fleshly body or one does not love him at all!

Mary, Minister of Consolation

I would like to conclude these reflections on the role of the Woman of Nazareth in the Church by saying something about how she ministers to each of us in our small, fragile existence, with our failures and losses. For good reason the holy People of God invoke the Mother of Jesus as *Refuge of Sinners* and *Consoler of the Afflicted.* Both these titles concern the experience of sorrow. The first one is about moral sorrow, that is, the experience of personal sin. The second is about specifically Christian sorrow, that is, the inevitable sufferings that come from following Christ.

Refuge of Sinners. Let's think about Mary's existential situation after the death of her Son. Beneath the cross, she became mother of the disciples. She stayed with them in the Cenacle, awaiting the promised Holy Spirit. Mary completes her earthly life in the community of Jerusalem. She, the Mother of the Messiah, the woman without sin, had to become a mother for those persons who had denied her Son. The Mother of God had to become the Mother of sinners. The Mother of the Holy One had to become the guardian of the unfaithful and cowardly. It's no small thing—and something hard for us to fathom—that Mary never had any evil in her heart. She saw everything from the outlook of grace. From her own experience, the Virgin well knew that the Almighty One does great things, because nothing is impossible to God. That is why she could remain in Jerusalem in prayer after the resurrection. God rewarded her with the great gift of seeing the most powerful action of the Spirit: to transform sinners into apostles.

Completely transparent to the Holy Spirit, Mary remains among us as the "Refuge of Sinners." Through her intercession, the dark past of the disciples was forgiven, and they emerged as new men, able to bring the Gospel to humanity. Each penitent Christian truly finds in Mary a refuge free from the cries of accusers. Then the devil, her eternal enemy, can no longer hurl himself as "accuser" on the conscience of the fallen one (see Rev 12:10). Many, even in the Church, are tempted to condemn without appeal those Christians who make mistakes (in an anti-evangelical return to pious Puritanism!). However, the Mother of Jesus remains the only one to always believe in the possibility of change and conversion, because she witnesses to the action of the Spirit, who transformed the traitor Peter into the prince of the apostles. In the Church, Mary is the minister of consolation, especially for those who feel lost, for impossible cases, for those who fail to live up to a commitment, who have not always fulfilled the mission entrusted to them, for all the so-called hopeless cases.

Consoler of the afflicted. Let us immediately make clear that the "afflicted" in the Gospel are especially those who know how to accept the inevitable suffering reserved for the followers of Jesus. The Master does not hide this reality from us: "If they persecuted me, they will persecute you" (Jn 15:20). "Woe to you when all speak well of you" (Lk 6:26). As we have already seen, Mary shared in the afflictions of Jesus, his rejection by the people. Simeon announced to her that she would share with her

> *Completely transparent to the Holy Spirit, Mary remains among us as the "Refuge of Sinners."*

Son the bread of sorrow, the rejection of a people who would first exalt him and then immediately consider him a cursed "sign that will be opposed" (Lk 2:34–35). But the Mother of Jesus is not only consoler of those who share her Son's rejection. She is also Mother of all who struggle to understand the Master's way of acting, when he seemed "out of himself" (see Mk 3:21), even while they continue to believe. Who better than Mary knows the dark night of faith? Or the struggle of those who have to give an account to God who turns things upside down, who first announces to her the regal greatness of his Son and then places her before his shameful end? Who "persuades by dissuading, draws by rejecting, acts in suffering, builds by destroying, and renders eternal by dying?"[10]

In the community of believers, Mary, above all, can be justly invoked as "consoler of the afflicted," for she experienced the joy that the Lord reserves for those who persevere with him in his trials. After the cross and the flight of the terrorized disciples, she observed their rebirth. Beyond the defeat of the Messiah, she experienced the victory of his disarmed love. The Spirit, the first consoler, consoled Mary and he continues to help us *through her*, giving to us the same consolation he showed her (see 2 Cor 1:4).

Summary

The Holy Spirit forms the flesh of the Son of God in the womb of a woman, and generates the Church in the womb of the Cenacle of Jerusalem. Every time the third person of the Trinity gives life to something new, Mary is present. Just as we cannot separate this Mother from her Son, so the experiences of Mary and of the Church are indissolubly united through the Spirit's generating action. The Church depends continually on the outpouring of the Spirit. This outpouring is constantly active if he is not saddened (see Eph 4:30), in other words, if he is told: "behold, here I am," as with the Virgin of Nazareth. Adoration

---

10. Pierre de Bérulle, *Le grandezze di Gesu,* op. cit., 18.

and silence are typical Marian attitudes and make of the Christian community the *new creation of the Paraclete*.

The Holy Spirit, the ineffable Person whom the human imagination cannot represent, finds in the Mother of the Lord a sort of mirror. Through her we can gather something, we can "babble" like children and see the features of his beauty by fixing our gaze on Mary. Even if it is said of the Spirit that we don't know where he comes from or where he goes (see Jn 3:8), in the Virgin Mary's story we perceive his voice in a gentle manner. As the Gospels attest, Mary lives those attitudes that are proper to one who is full of the Spirit: the praise born from knowing how to see the action of God in history, the prophecy that bursts forth from the intimate presence of Christ, and the freedom of discipleship.

First in the Communion of Saints by her faith, her hope, and her total and gratuitous love, the Mother of the Lord extends her spiritual presence to the Church of all times. Her presence passes through her *virginal maternity*, the paradigm of how the Church can generate new children in virtue of the Holy Spirit and not human effort. Her royal presence guides us in obeying the Son. Finally, as spiritual Mother of the baptized, Mary invokes upon them the Spirit who generates and makes the interior person grow unto the full stature of Christ.

For the believer the Woman of Nazareth is also the unequivocal memory of the Lord's incarnation and passion. Mary's son, Jesus, is truly human, real, and lived in the flesh. A disincarnate or a spiritualistic Christianity can't stand up to the test when Jesus' Mother is present. She always nails us to fidelity to history and responsibility toward the earthly life that providence has given us. In addition to the *ministry of Christian realism,* Mary also echoes the consolation of the Spirit. Mary knew the stupidity of evil found in human frailty, and she experienced firsthand the obscurity of faith.

Mary, then, is our "refuge" when we open the door to repentance, and she is our comfort when we are tempted to believe that rebirth is impossible after Calvary.

Meditations

The *Church "becomes* herself *a mother* by accepting God's word with fidelity" (*LG,* 64). Like Mary, who first believed by accepting the Word of God revealed to her at the annunciation and by remaining faithful to that word in all her trials even unto the cross, so too the Church becomes a mother when, *accepting with fidelity the Word of God,* "by her preaching and by Baptism *she brings forth to a new and immortal life children* who are conceived *of the Holy Spirit* and born of God" (*LG,* 64). This "maternal" characteristic of the Church was expressed in a particularly vivid way by the apostle to the Gentiles when he wrote: "My little children, with whom I am again in travail until Christ be formed in you!" (Gal 4:19). . . .

It can be said that from Mary the Church also learns her own motherhood: she recognizes the maternal dimension of her vocation, which is essentially bound to her sacramental nature, in "contemplating Mary's mysterious sanctity, imitating her charity and faithfully fulfilling the Father's will" (*LG,* 64). If the Church is the sign and instrument of intimate union with God, she is so by reason of her motherhood, because, receiving life from the Spirit, she "generates" sons and daughters of the human race to a new life in Christ. For, just as *Mary is at the service of the mystery of the Incarnation,* so *the Church* is always *at the service of the mystery of adoption to sonship* through grace. . . .

Given Mary's relationship to the Church as an exemplar, the Church is close to her and seeks to become like her: "Imitating the Mother of her Lord, and by the power of the Holy Spirit, she preserves with virginal purity an integral faith, a firm hope, and a sincere charity" (*LG,* 64). Mary is thus present in the mystery of the Church as a *model.* But the Church's mystery also consists in generating people to a new and immortal life: this is her motherhood in the Holy Spirit. And here Mary is not only the model and figure of the Church; she is much more. For *"with maternal love she cooperates in the birth and development"* of the sons and daughters of Mother Church. The Church's motherhood is accomplished not only according to the model and figure of the Mother of God but also with her "cooperation." The Church *draws* abundantly from this cooperation, that is to say from the maternal mediation which is characteristic of Mary, insofar as already on earth she cooperated in the rebirth and development of the Church's sons and daughters, as the Mother of that Son whom the Father "placed as the firstborn among many brethren" (*LG,* 63).

She cooperated, as the Second Vatican Council teaches, with a maternal love (see *LG,* 63). Here we perceive the real value of the words spoken by Jesus to his Mother at the hour of the cross: "Woman, behold your son" and to the disciple: "Behold your mother" (Jn 19:26–27). They are words which determine *Mary's place in the life of Christ's disciples* and they express—as I have already said—the new motherhood of the Mother of the Redeemer: a spiritual motherhood, born from the heart of the Paschal Mystery of the Redeemer of the world. It is a motherhood in the order of grace, for it implores the gift of the Spirit, who raises up the new children of God, redeems through the sacrifice of Christ: that Spirit whom, together with the Church, Mary too received on the day of Pentecost.

Saint John Paul II, Encyclical Letter
Mother of the Redeemer (Redemptoris Mater)
March 25, 1987, no. 43–44

Besides this, since Jesus is the Fruit of Mary now just as much as ever—as heaven and earth repeat thousands and thousands of times a day, "and Blessed be the fruit of thy womb, Jesus"—it is certain that Jesus Christ is, for each person in particular who possesses him, as truly the fruit of the work of Mary, as he is for the whole world in general. If anyone of the faithful has Jesus Christ formed in his heart, he can say boldly, "All thanks be to Mary! what I possess is her effect and her fruit, and without her I should never have had it." We can apply to her more truly than Saint Paul applied to himself those words—"My little children, for whom I am again in the pain of childbirth until Christ is formed in you" (Gal 4:19). [Mary says:] "I am in labor again with all the children of God, until Jesus Christ my Son be formed in them in the fullness of his age."

Saint Augustine, surpassing himself, and going beyond all I have said, affirms that all the predestined, in order to be conformed to the image of the Son of God, are hidden in this world in the womb of the most holy Virgin. There they are guarded, nourished, brought up, and helped to grow by that good Mother until she has brought them forth to glory after death, which is properly the day of their birth, as the Church calls the death of the just. O mystery of grace, unknown to the lost and but little known even to the predestined!

God the Holy Spirit wishes to form himself in her, and to form the chosen ones for himself by her. He has said to her, "My well-beloved and my spouse, implant the roots of all your virtues in my chosen ones, so that they may grow from virtue to virtue, and from grace to grace. I took so much delight in you when you lived on earth and practiced the most sublime virtues, that I still desire to find you on earth, without your ceasing to be in heaven. For this purpose, reproduce yourself in my chosen ones, that I may see in them with joy the roots of your invincible faith, your profound humility, your total self-control, your sublime prayer, your ardent charity, your firm hope, and all your virtues. You are always my spouse, as faithful, pure, and fruitful as ever. Let your faith give me faithful ones; let your purity give me virgins, and let your fertility give me my temples and my chosen ones."

When Mary has put down her roots in a soul, she produces in it marvels of grace, which she alone can produce, because she alone is the fruitful Virgin. She never has had, and never will have, her equal in purity and in fruitfulness.

Together with the Holy Spirit, Mary has produced the greatest wonder that has been or ever will be—the God-Man. Consequently she will produce the greatest wonders that will come about in the latter times. The formation and education of the great saints who will come at the end of the world are reserved for her. For it is only that singular and miraculous Virgin who can produce, in union with the Holy Spirit, singular and extraordinary things.

When the Holy Spirit, her spouse, finds Mary in a soul, he flies there and fully enters into it. He communicates himself to that soul abundantly, according to the extent that the soul makes room for its spouse. One of the main reasons why the Holy Spirit does not now do startling wonders in our souls is because he does not find there a sufficiently close union with his faithful and inseparable spouse. I say inseparable spouse, because ever since [the Holy Spirit], that Substantial Love of the Father and the Son, espoused Mary in order to form Jesus Christ, the Head of the elect, and Jesus Christ in the elect, He has never repudiated her, inasmuch as she has always been fruitful and faithful.

Saint Louis Grignion de Montfort,
True Devotion, nn. 33–36

Mary communicates life especially in three ongoing stages:

At Nazareth she conceived us. Our spiritual conception happened in the mystery of the incarnation. Without the incarnation we would still be buried in the death of sin. Now God has worked the incarnation through Mary, and willed that her participation be free, conscious, and necessary.

Her *"fiat"* was an act of consent for our supernatural conception and for her motherhood in our regard.

She generated us on Calvary. The mystery of the incarnation finds its fulfillment in the mystery of the redemption. Through his own death Christ merited for us to live definitively of his life. That which was came to the light.[11]

Consequently, just as our spiritual begetting began in the mystery of the incarnation and received its fulfillment in the Redemption, so Mary's spiritual maternity, which started at Nazareth, was brought to fulfillment and proclaimed on Calvary.

---

11. Literal translation of the Italian. The thought seems to be drawn from Saint John's Gospel, "What has come into being in him was life, and the life was the light of all people" (Jn 1:4). —*Ed.*

She generates us one by one at the baptismal font. The baptismal font is, for each one of us, Bethlehem. From a supernatural point of view, we are, at birth, stillborn. That life, which was merited for all by Christ's death, needs to be infused in each one of us. It is Mary who undertakes this role. The son of man becomes thus a son of God.

The archangel Gabriel greeted her as "full of grace." The Church's ordinary teaching understood this to mean that Mary is the Mediatrix and distributor of the grace won by Jesus Christ with the cooperation of Mary.

Blessed James Alberione[12]

---

12. *Ut Perfectus Sit Homo Dei*, Instruction X, "Mary, Disciple and Teacher," 506–507.

CHAPTER THREE

Live Mary to Give Christ

"God chose what is weak in the world to shame the strong" (1 Cor 1:27).

———— • • • ————

Consecrated to the Living One in Mary

The Baptism we have received places us in the vital space of Christ: in him we breathe, we move, we think, we love (see Acts 17:28). A seed of eternal life is transplanted into our soul, so that it might grow to maturity and reach every fiber of our being. Baptism is a dynamic reality. It catapults us onto the raceway of a stadium where we are surrounded by saints cheering us on. We don't run for a gold medal, but toward a merciful Father who awaits us with open arms. He wants us to participate in the glory of his Son, Jesus, the author and perfecter of faith, who first ran that race to the finish to open a way for us (see Heb 12:1–2).

We will never cease to be amazed at what this first sacrament works within us. In the womb of Mary, human nature and divine nature were united for the first time. Similarly, in the baptismal font—a true Marian icon—the Spirit of Christ bonds indissolubly with our flesh. The miracle of the incarnation is [in a sense][1] repeated in the human person. In the framework of a birth without time, Baptism makes the created person a participant in the whole pathway of Christ from Bethlehem to the Kingdom of heaven, but not without passing through the cross and the silence of Holy Saturday.[2]

The Baptismal Journey: Starting Point and Goal

In Baptism we are *consecrated* to the Lord and to him alone. Our life belongs to him, and his life is transfused into us for eternity. We are told *whose* we are, even before knowing *who* we are, because only in the loving belonging to a reality can we discover

---

1. The words in brackets are added to clarify that there is a difference between the incarnation of the Word and our participation in this mystery by grace. Baptism enables us to become adopted children of God by grace, whereas Jesus is the Son of God by nature. —*Ed.*

2. "Our rebirth in baptism is therefore symbolized in the birth which, overshadowed by the Spirit, gave us the Redeemer born of the Virgin." Hugo Rahner, *Our Lady and the Church* (Bethesda, MD: Zaccheus Press), 2004, 65.

the real face of the person. Made holy by the Spirit, we have the grace to cling to the mystical journey of Jesus. He *relives* this existential event in those who begin the journey of life from the baptismal font. The departure point and the goal of this *Christifying dynamic*, which Paul masterfully treats in his letters, are placed before us by two modern dogmas concerning the Virgin Mary. It is as if the Holy Spirit wanted to put right before our eyes the two sure goals of our solemn procession into the divine. What are the mysteries of the Immaculate Conception and the assumption if not the theological description of the two focal points of the journey?

In the Immaculate Conception, God preserved Mary from original sin. In Baptism we are freed from the fault of the fall of our first parents. Then the same "fullness of grace" given to the Woman of Nazareth is bestowed also on us.[3] For Mary it was a singular grace of pardon that preserved her from original sin, communicated to her in view of her most unique mission as Mother of God. For us it is a grace of pardon that sanctifies us and prepares us to become "mothers and fathers" in the faith for others. But in both cases the same music resounds. God gives grace always in view of a mission, of a duty. He does not grant private gifts but riches to be shared! No matter at what stage we

---

3. This can be understood in the sense that we too receive sanctifying grace in baptism, but in a lesser degree than Mary, for Catholic teaching holds that Mary received a unique grace of holiness: "The Father blessed Mary more than any other created person 'in Christ with every spiritual blessing in the heavenly places'" (*CCC*, no. 492). —*Ed.*

find ourselves in the Christian way of life—whether beginners or advanced—we always have to return to the *grace of the origins*, whose name is always and only *Mercy*. The mercy that the Lord extends to "those who fear him" (Lk 1:50)—and thus on Mary as on each of us—is not just the *beginning* but rather the basis of our existence. It allows us to remain small and reminds us that we are nothing and what we do would remain nothing!

In the dogma of the Immaculate Conception, the beginning of the baptismal journey of Christification is not only recounted but also assigned as an approach, a way of proceeding, a destiny. Everything is always and only mercy, from the beginning to the end, from youth to old age. Mary's holiness dwells precisely in her clear awareness of the divine goodness given to her from the moment of her conception until the sunset of her earthly life. In her the mercy of God could work freely from the beginning to the end, since she put no obstacles or stumbling blocks to its irradiation (like a ray of sunlight crossing the most pure air). But in us the spreading of that same mercy has to do with pardon of sin, always granted in the "second baptism" of sacramental confession. To correspond to the grace that pardons is the permanent state of the baptized person, who, even after reaching the heights of the mystical life, remains simply a beloved sinner, "a condemned person who no longer experiences any shame."[4]

In the assumption of the Blessed Virgin, on the other hand, we contemplate the destiny that awaits us, the goal to be reached:

---

4. John Climacus, *The Ladder of Divine Ascent,* Discourse V.

the resurrection of the body. "But God, who is rich in mercy, out of the great love with which he loved us even when we were dead through our trespasses, made us alive together with Christ—by grace you have been saved—and raised us up with him and seated us with him in the heavenly places in Christ Jesus" (Eph 2:4–6).

Baptism gives us eternal life, not success or human respect. It's good to keep in mind that we are not Christians for a generic afterlife but for heaven. Precisely in view of this destination, everything we experience in life is precious. For the baptized, to think about the things above (see Col 3:1–2) is not to flee from reality but to grasp the profound truth of the world. Every creature, every person,

Everything is always and only mercy, from the beginning to the end, from youth to old age.

and even animals and inanimate objects are streams of a fountain that bursts up in a sealed place that we will one day inherit. Nothing helps us to live earthly life with more enthusiasm than the thought of heaven; nothing else helps us find the Font hidden in all things. In view of this future hope, the baptized person is not merely someone who uses creation but who *contemplates* its beauty. In Mary assumed into heaven, all the goodness of creation (even under its tragic aspects of sickness and of death), which came forth from the hands of God, will return forever into the hands of the Artist and under his serene gaze.

But the profound meaning of the mystery is rooted here: What does the Father want returned to his hands? Simply the Christ, the only Beloved, hidden in all things! And us in him. In this light the journey of the baptized lies completely in allowing the Spirit to work, the "finger of God's right hand" (see the hymn, *Veni Creator Spiritus*). After having scraped impurities off the canvas, with the grace of pardon, the Spirit paints on me the clear face of the beloved Son, which he offers to the Father with perfect love. Then after my death, I will be recognized by him so that I may enter the endless joy of the Creator's contented gaze. The key of heaven is conformity to Christ. Mary enters there immediately, the exceptional first fruits of the resurrection, for Jesus lives in her perfectly. Jesus is transfused in Mary, and in her the Father is well pleased to admire the features of his Beloved. As Saint Louis de Montfort exclaims, the Virgin in paradise is "the paradise of God." The Father reposes in her and rejoices as he did on the seventh day of creation (see Gen 2:3).

Consecrated to Jesus "in" Mary

The riches of Baptism are right before our eyes. What I have attempted to describe is only a pale outline of the mystery we are immersed in, because human words cannot fully describe divine realities. The limits of language! That said, we must seek to understand where Mary fits within this dynamic. To do this, let us go back for a moment along the pathway of the Word. Although being equal to God, the Word did not consider his divinity as "something to be exploited," but emptied himself of everything, to become not a powerful or privileged man but a *servant*. This descent of the Word into created things reached the depths of humanity, even to the point of letting himself be numbered among criminals and outcasts on the cross (see Phil 2:5–9). *Kenosis* is the key to the pathway of Jesus: the self-abasement by which he empties himself. And only after having touched bottom does the Master rise to the glory of the Father. Abasement and exaltation, self-emptying and triumph. No other concepts come close to the Christian mystery. It is the eternal wisdom of God![5]

Let us return to Baptism. As we have already observed, to be baptized means to surrender oneself to Christ. And Christ wants to live in me, in his mysteries (see Gal 2:20), even to the point of involving me in his return to the Father in glory after death. But this pathway, to be authentically his, has to pass through his own *kenosis*. Therefore, if we neglect this *dominant Christological clue*, we will not live his existence but will be pretending to live the Christian life! Taking on this way of thinking, however, is left to my freedom and remains the great invitation of the Master: "If any want to become my followers, let them deny themselves and take up their cross and follow me" (Mt 16: 24). Baptism is an absolute grace, but its vivifying efficacy is left to my free choice in accepting it! We could say that through Baptism Christ is conceived in me, but he grows and develops in me through the

---

5. For more on this topic of the self-emptying/exultation, see the book by the late Montfort Father, Stefano De Fiores, *Maria Madre di Gesù, Sintesi storico-salvifica* (Bologna: EDB, 2002), 212–33.

continual and free acceptance of grace. If I refuse or withdraw, this conception could even end in rejecting the life of Christ in me.

The way I see it, in this free acceptance of the *kenosis* of the Master, we find the consecration to Jesus *in* Mary. I choose to entrust myself to the Mother to recognize myself, like her, as a servant of the Lord. I become a creature with a serene awareness of my own nothingness, pleasing to the Father. In that way *choosing for me the humility and abasement of Mary, the Holy Spirit finds in the space of my interiority the possibility of allowing the power of Baptism to act completely to its depths*. This is the profound grace of entrustment to the Virgin.

> *To consecrate oneself to Mary involves espousing her humility, to put the old self to death.*

Let us consider this theme with Pauline language, to deepen it from a complementary point of view. The Apostle recalls that with Baptism we are immersed in the death of Christ, to rise with him to new life. This doesn't happen once and for all, but day by day. In every moment we can choose to die to ourselves (to our illusory ideas, egocentric interests, pleasures that don't bear fruit) in order to cause the new self to grow. To consecrate oneself to Mary involves espousing her humility, to put the old self to death. At the same time, it means to receive, through her intercession, the Holy Spirit who creates the new self. As Saint Louis de Montfort well understood, by giving ourselves to

Mary, we accept and we choose with full awareness our baptismal commitment as the primary occupation in life. To destroy the *ego* means to build the divine *You*, emptying ourselves of self to be reclothed in Christ (see Eph 4:24).

True Devotion

Having said all this, we can tranquilly affirm that true devotion to Mary consists in choosing to let the Holy Spirit work freely in us. It means giving him space with the humility that (other than being the *sine qua non* of Christianity) is the uncontestable feature of the Virgin Mother's own way of loving the Lord: "No saint learned the humility of Jesus more perfectly than Mary, his mother, because no one participated as intimately in the knowledge and love of our Lord. Near him she saw the reasons for being humble with a vision that was clear, continual, and penetrating. We lose sight of this, we forget, but she never did!"[6]

To consecrate oneself to Mary is not a passing fashion, a spiritual hobby, but a ready response to the gift of the dying Jesus: "Here is your mother" (Jn 19:27). We don't need to distrust the gifts of God, for he knows what we need before we even ask him (see Mt 6:8). Perhaps no one has seen this act of Jesus in a theological and symbolic framework as well as Saint Louis de Montfort. For this great French apostle, baptized persons must cast themselves like raw clay into the "form" of Mary so that the

6. L. Beaudenom, *L'ultimo di tutti (Mk 9:35). Formazione all'umilta* (Rome: Edizioni Casa di Nazareth), 171.

Spirit might form them.[7] The form does not impress its own image but that of Christ, because the Mother is the "mold" of the Son. We take on the "form," which is Mary, in order to assume the features of Jesus and thus bring to perfection our own baptismal pathway.[8]

———•••———

True devotion to Mary consists in choosing to let the Holy Spirit work freely in us.

———•••———

And so the miracle of the incarnation of the Word is repeated mystically in us. As he took form in Mary, now Jesus takes form in us. This happens on the condition that we agree to make our own the Virgin Mary's humble receptivity to the movements of the Spirit. But what does it mean concretely to enter into the form that is Mary? How can we place ourselves into a suitable spiritual climate?

---

7. *The Secret of Mary,* nn. 16–17.

8. In this sense, profession of the evangelical counsels of poverty, chastity, and obedience, and the consecration to Mary, although not the same, as Cardinal de Bérulle believed, are perfectly complementary. Both find their theological foundation in Baptism; both have the purpose of Christification of the person. In my opinion, Marian consecration, representing the acceptance of the gift of the disciple by Mary (which is a definitive act recapitulated in Jesus, Spouse and Lord) is in a "mystical" sense superior to the profession of the counsels, which are directed, instead, to following the style of life of the Jesus of history. I stress the "mystical" superiority of the consecration to Jesus through Mary, and certainly not that of the canonical or theological aspect of public vows.

The wisdom of Saint Louis de Montfort again comes to our aid. Drawing from some of his texts, we can find practical pointers for a serious spiritual journey that rests in the reality of the flesh—the great ideal of baptismal consecration lived in Mary. Saint Louis de Montfort writes that interior devotion to the Virgin is concretized in a lived Christian life *"by means of— with—in—through"* Mary.[9] Note that these four prepositions are not juxtaposed. Their order indicates a progressive and ascending pathway that we can follow with much good will and only by the grace of God. I will seek to offer a contemporary interpretation of these "states of the soul."

To live by means of Mary means to accept the "means" through which the Mother of Jesus experienced the Son being formed in her womb. This is the first step of true devotion; without it the others are not possible. This *means,* which always formed and accompanied Mary, is the Holy Spirit. To live alongside Mary means not to choose any other light but that of the Consoler. The Spirit who descended upon her at the annunciation is the same One who works in me and who wants to generate a new self. Here we touch a delicate point in the spiritual life: many people believe that to live in the Spirit means simply to do good. But this is not enough. To truly live in the Spirit, we need to be directed to choosing what is more pleasing to God and *more perfect* for me (see Rom 12:2), not simply what is good. Some persons may be great

---

9. See *The Secret of Mary,* nn. 43–49; *Treatise on True Devotion,* nn. 257–265.

ascetics, others completely given to prayer, while others may serve
the poor or teach theology. But if one does not keep their ears
open with right intention to the suggestions of the Spirit, he or she
will inevitably sadden the Spirit (see Eph 4:30). The great conversion of our Christian existence lies in resolving to follow the Spirit,
in making ourselves his servants, in choosing what he suggests to
us. By means of Mary, we live through the Spirit who possessed
and moved her. Mary did not limit herself to observing the law of
Israel. She was ready to go beyond the law when the Spirit moved
her toward unexpected, unusual dimensions. She understood this
by attentive observation of events and the uprightness of her free
heart. Perhaps this is the most difficult point of true devotion to
Mary. We can love her silence and hiddenness, but how difficult it
is to go where the Spirit leads us—renouncing our beautiful projects and missionary dreams (which we always seek for the good of
others!). How fatiguing it is for the person who is not pure of heart
to renounce ill-advised zeal and to dedicate him or herself to the
work of the Spirit that might be hidden or seem unsuccessful.

To live with Mary: It is necessary to unite ourselves to our
Mother's intentions, which are the same as those of Jesus. The
Son lives for the glory of the Father, and this glory on earth is the
invocation in the Our Father: "hallowed be your name." The
intention of Jesus and of Mary is simply that the *name of God* be
magnified, that everyone recognize and experience God's fidelity
and mercy. The Lord willed only this throughout his life. His
mother followed him not only physically, but also by making her
own his deepest desire: "Father, glorify your name" (Jn 12:28).
To live with Mary means to assimilate this straining toward the

glory of God, repeating incessantly: "Not to us, O LORD, not to us, but to your name give glory" (Ps 115:1). People think that they will win happiness by making themselves "gods," almost as if to rob glory from the Creator. They don't understand that peace of heart is acquired only in serenely accepting what it means to be a creature, full of the limitations and weaknesses that the good Father has assigned to each one of us. The glory of God is our peace. Mary lived this way, saying her yes to the good will of the One who serenely gazes on all those who humbly surrender to his tenderness. This challenging point could be summed up completely in the invitation to espouse the *humble faith* of the handmaiden of the Lord.

• • •

Silence is a necessary medicine for growing in the spiritual life.

• • •

To live in Mary: We need to enter the "cell" of her humble silence, almost to disappear in it mystically, following the example of Jesus who hid himself in Mary for nine months. God does not speak in noise. When we imagine he communicates to us in anxiety of heart, we risk being profoundly disappointed. Silence is necessary, whether it be a formal silence when we refrain from speaking and listening to words (most of which are useless at best), or an interior silence of a tranquil mind that stops running wild with endless thoughts. Silence is a necessary medicine for growing in the spiritual life. You can't listen to God if you don't stop listening to yourself. It is often said that Mary's life was spent in silence; the Gospels give us very few of her words! But that doesn't tell us much about her way. Rather, as Bérulle observes, she teaches *transformative silence.* The silence of Mary is not a mental vacuum but an exercise of faith. In place of our thousands of thoughts, she substitutes the rock of the word, even when not completely understood or when facts seem to contradict it. To use a summary image of this "living in Mary" we could take advantage of a place: Nazareth! There the Virgin exercised a humble and meditative silence. It was *humble* because it was nourished by the ordinary, daily things that do not shine; and it was *meditative* because it transformed everything into an object of contemplation. To convert ourselves to Nazareth is to finally commit ourselves to communicate with God starting from *my reality*, whatever it may be. It means renouncing deceptive dreams and unfounded fears, so we can exclaim as Jacob did at Bethel: "Surely the LORD is in this place—and I did not know it" (Gen 28:16).

To live for Mary: Finally, true devotion teaches us to live with trust in the spiritual maternity of the Virgin Mary. It should be stressed that we must want to live only for God. He alone is enough. But we do not come before the Lord as solitary heroes or anti-social adventurers. Rather, we stand in communion with the other baptized Christians and with all the saints, past and present. For this reason, we turn away from an elite, individualistic vision of life in the Spirit. We convert ourselves to an ecclesial way of sanctity, which, unfortunately, is often reduced to the individual sanctity of certain beautiful souls. The expression "to live for Mary" takes nothing away from dedication to the person of Christ. Rather, it adds a communitarian dimension. In that sense the expression is the twin of the other: "to live for the Church." We dedicate our lives for the Church and in it to Mary, the first fruits of the Church. We entrust ourselves to one another, to respond to the twofold command of the Lord, "Whoever listens to you listens to me," and, "Here is your mother" (Lk 10:16; Jn 19:27). The miracle at Cana of Galilee is an extremely rich lesson that helps us understand what it means to "live for Mary." As the servants entrusted themselves to her invitation, through her we also make ourselves ready for service at the wedding feast the Master celebrates with his people. Our Christian action bursts forth from the invitation of the Virgin: "Do whatever he tells you" (Jn 2:5). Further, in the mind of Saint Louis de Montfort, "living for Mary" also includes a decisive missionary aspect. It is a matter of communicating to others the evangelical and dogmatic content that concerns her, inasmuch as the Virgin is "the mysterious environment and easy" means to meet Christ. To make known Mary's exemplary life would be to give people the gift of the loving and proper form of baptismal existence. This is the ultimate goal of true devotion: service in the Church and announcing the Gospel.

To Feel with the Church: Verification of True Devotion

We have just noted that true devotion to the Mother of the Lord leads us to serve the Church. Often this devotion is understood to reduce Marian spirituality to something merely personal or that, at most, has a strong impact on an individual. Nothing is further from the truth! The journey of consecration to Jesus in Mary puts the grace of Baptism to work in our own spiritual life. Thus, it must lead us into service. This happens not because by doing this we become good or capable, but because by living *in* Mary, we allow the Holy Spirit to form Christ in us. Because Jesus is the missionary of the Father (see Heb 3:1), if we are truly receptive to the grace of Baptism, we too become transformed into missionaries of the Kingdom. It is not simply a matter of learning skills, but of a true and real *Christic form.* The mission, the authentic mission, is a matter of mystics, not of technical know-how! We will return to this topic. For now, I wish only to underline the ecclesial dimension of devotion to Mary: to live in her involves living the Church, feeling the Church as a true mother, and serving her as children, not as poorly paid employees.

> *True devotion to the Mother of the Lord leads us to serve the Church.*

We can almost identify the emotional world of a mother and child in the first years of life. Nothing interrupts the immediate empathy that allows a woman to understand what her baby needs. The Virgin of Nazareth lived a holy symbiosis with Jesus. Mary perceived this union emotionally, even when she did not intellectually understand. After the death of her Son, Mary's capacity to be so closely involved with her Son was transferred to the newborn community, to its fears and uncertainties. As Luke testifies, Mary is at the heart of the mystical body of Christ with her assiduous prayer and with her praise (see Acts 1:14; 2:46–47). That being noted, nothing more is said about her; the silence of Scripture is total! Her existence is lost in that of the Church, almost as if it is no longer necessary to speak of her singularly, inasmuch as it is a matter of two inseparable events. True devotion to Mary is not placed before the Church but *in* the Church. It would be absurd to consecrate oneself to the Mother of Christ and then stay on the margins of the Christian community. It would be as absurd and ridiculous as a man who wanted only to marry a woman's soul without also loving her body! The one who lives Mary lives equally *by means* of the Church's sacraments, grows in faith with the brethren, loves and thinks *in* the Church, and builds the community with his or her dedication, working *for* the Gospel.

However, we must not be naive or complacent. It's one thing to give ourselves to Mary, the woman without stain of sin; it's another thing to stay in the Church, loving her for what she is, but above all for what she is destined to become. Some people live in the community simply to gain advantages from it, even on the affective level. The need to be recognized suffocates their generosity and peace. The presence of these brothers and sisters is much more harmful for the Church than those people who do not even want to hear a word about the Church. It is not rare that people who have not achieved the power they wanted in their social life or at work use all their energies in a "service" to the community, but with a badly hidden intention of starting over again in life. Before these false motivations, from which none of us can presume ourselves exempt (including the author!), Mary teaches us how we need to stay in the Church without personal interests or ulterior motives. The image is clear: on Calvary, at that moment when the Messiah generated his community from his pierced side, Mary again found herself losing all that she held most precious, as Abraham had with his son Isaac on Mount Moriah (see Gen 22). The beloved Son was about to die, but he did not allow her to close herself up in sorrow. In fact, he entrusted his beloved disciple to her, relaunching and reorienting her maternal dedication in an unexpected way. This is the final miracle of Jesus: to cause the sorrow of his Mother to become not a wall against but a door open to love. So the Mother of the Lord, a widow about to lose her only Son, represents Jerusalem. After having contemplated the servant of God emptied even unto death, Jerusalem exalts in joy because the children of the abandoned wife have become more numerous than those of the espoused woman (see Isa 53–54).

This suffering for the Church, this Marian sorrow opens us to generative love without expectations. This sorrow is the *only serious way of staying in the community*, even when some of its members scandalize us, or when we encounter widespread anti-evangelical attitudes. At the foot of these crosses that egoism often plants on the terrain of the community, outrage or censures do no good. But a Marian presence can transform the sorrow of scandal into an occasion of healing and rebirth to a sincere evangelical way of life.

The "Marian" Style of Giving Christ

"Do not be afraid to take Mary as your wife, for the child conceived in her is from the Holy Spirit" (Mt 1:20). The angel's invitation to Joseph of Nazareth is now given to us. To live Mary. To enter into that ineffable intimacy with her, where the treasures of wisdom are enclosed, means putting ourselves totally and unconditionally under the dominion of the Holy Spirit, who *generates* Christ in us. In the "Mariform"[10] dimension of Baptism, all our little deaf and mute idols (even those speciously good or religious), are put out in the open and reveal their radical antagonism toward God. Mary brings out our aversions to God. We often invoke Mary as the "one who destroyed all the heresies in the whole world" (inasmuch as the Marian dogmas are a guarantee of Catholic orthodoxy). Yet we should not forget that before being outside, the dangerous "heretic" is within us. We can all subtly slip toward an erroneous praxis in life, because of original sin. We are masters at camouflaging our own malice and pretending that only what pertains to our personal interests also pertains to the glory of God. To join Mary on the way of the Gospel helps us to reveal the truth about the little idols that we carry in our pockets. It forces us to bring them out, to put them under the light of God's justice. True Marian spirituality does not distance

---

10. This expression is from the Flemish theologian Michele di Sant' Agostino (1621–1684), a Carmelite of the Ancient Observance, and author of a short treatise: *Da vita mariaeformi et mariana in Maria propter Mariam* (1669).

us from Christ, but puts him at the center of our heart without any competition. It is not by chance, perhaps, that the Order of the Brothers of the Most Blessed Virgin Mary of Mount Carmel, dedicated to Mary invoked as "Sister" and "Lady of the Place," identify their origins with that triumph of the Prophet Elijah over the prophets of Baal (see 1 Kings 18:20–40). Where the Mother is, one lives under the Lordship of the Son without plausible alternatives.

We further discover that to receive Mary in our interior house is, in a certain sense, *very dangerous*. If we accept her with sincerity, we must serenely resolve that nothing will remain of our old self! In my view this is a true theological principle. To explain better: so that the incarnation would happen in her womb, the Virgin was *pre*-redeemed in the first instant of her conception.[11] In her heart grace worked the miracle of reestablishing the crystalline and exclusive friendship with God that Adam and Eve had before sin. A clear principle of the spiritual life derives from that dogmatic truth: we can conceive Jesus in the temple of our body in the measure that we allow the Spirit to take away everything that is not only harmful but also superfluous. Therefore the most beautiful request that the devotee of Mary can make is to ask the Lord to come into his or her own life and cast away everything that would cause him or her to walk

---

11. The dogma of the Immaculate Conception means that Mary "was redeemed from the moment of her conception" in view of the merits of Christ, the Redeemer of the world (see *CCC* nos. 490–493). —*Ed.*

"with one foot in two shoes." Jesus did exactly that on that memorable day in Jerusalem when he cast out from the Temple the merchants who had reduced the holy place to a den of thieves (see Mk 11:17).

With this as a premise, by way of preamble, we will again ask the question: Why didn't the dying Jesus entrust his Church to a powerful person, to a priest, rather than to a poor widow, his mother? What did he want to tell us with such an act?

The Covenant with Mary: Cross and Struggle

Perhaps in his agony Jesus put the Church into Mary's hands to teach us that the community must make *a covenant with her in order to reach the goal of fulfilling the Church's specific mission.*[12]

The Virgin Mary had a charge: to act in such a way that the Church be formed in the Spirit according to the form of "virgin mother," to continue to give the world the true life that comes from the Son. The apostolate of Mary in the times of salvation awaits collaborators. Let us make a covenant with her so that the Kingdom of God might come, so that people will find peace in their disquiet, resting on the heart of Christ! Those who find themselves associated to the mission of the Mother of the

---

12. The theme of an "alliance with Mary" was the focus of Blessed William Chaminade (1761–1850), the Founder of the Marianists Fathers, the Society of Mary. See J. B. Armbruster, *Conoscere, amare, servire Maria alla scuola di Padre Chaminade* (Milan, Cinisello Balsamo: Ed. Paoline, 1987), 99–157.

Redeemer must know this: to ally oneself with her for the Kingdom means taking on two perspectives, the cross and struggle.

The Crucified One willed to reveal to us the secret of success. It is not by chance that on Golgotha he says "behold," turning toward his Mother and the beloved disciple (see Jn 19:26–27). In Scripture the word "behold' introduces something new, a revelation. During Jesus' trial, Pilate, the unconscious presenter of the glory of God, revealed to the people the true model to follow: "Behold the man!" (Jn 19:5). In that beaten and humiliated being, the figure of the Servant of God shone forth, the Spouse of Israel ready to give his life for his bride. And so, while Pilate presented the Bridegroom to us in the praetorium, on Calvary Jesus showed us the face of the Bride in Mary. What a marvelous scene! Only the Woman learns that the Bridegroom gives his life for her, because she is given to contemplate the secret source of love: the cross, the apex of divine wisdom, the paradigm of every transmission of grace.

In other words, I should say that Jesus entrusted us to the hands of Mary to teach us that one can give the life of grace only by dying to self. As Mary became "mother" once again by accepting the loss of her Son, so we become generators of life by accepting the loss of ourselves. *To lose in order to give* is therefore the fundamental law of the maternity of Mary and of the Church. Whoever wants to evangelize with her cannot but hold to this crucified form, as Paul did with the Corinthians: "When I came to you, brothers and sisters, I did not come proclaiming the mystery of God to you in lofty words or wisdom. For I decided to know nothing among you except Jesus Christ, and him crucified" (1 Cor 2:1–2). The cross and fruitfulness are inseparable!

Naturally this is not easy, especially for two reasons: first, many Christians want to evangelize but without renouncing power and privilege; second, in today's environment the proclamation of salvation meets powerful anti-evangelical currents, whether conscious or not, where the enemy of human nature, the Evil One, sows victims very easily. This is the *mystery of iniquity* that manifests itself either as indifference, or as hate, or as mere rejection of the Lord (the Apostle Paul knew very well this "mystery of lawlessness": see 2 Thes 2:7). So we arrive at the second character, the ambient or attitude of Mary's mission. To make a covenant with the Mother of Jesus requires not only a "crucified" style of fruitfulness, but also the serene acceptance of struggle. That struggle always accompanies the seasons of the pilgrim Church.

In symbolic language the Book of Revelation (chapter 12) describes the difficulties of the newborn Christian community caught between temptations and persecutions. The sacred author's description is highly evocative. A woman appears in heaven, clothed in the sun as only God could have dressed her. The moon under her feet is a sign of the dominion over time that the moon measures. The crown of twelve stars on her head alludes to the twelve tribes of Israel and to the new people of Jesus, founded on the new covenant. The woman is pregnant and wails with birth pangs. However, it is not the serene peace of Bethlehem that reigns. A dragon waits nearby with open fangs to devour the baby when the woman gives birth. The dragon is the enemy of God and of his creation, who ruins the beauty of the world. The dragon devours humanity with his deceits and tears the sky, causing the stars fall to the earth like meteorites. Those fixed stars are like pearls in heaven from the hand of God, the splendid archive of his hidden designs (see Bar 3:34–35).

To make a covenant with Mary is not some devout game; it means taking our part in the struggle between the New Eve and the dragon!

Clearly, this dragon refers to the serpent of Genesis. Even in that first book of origins, this perverse and cunning creature, who sees things in a base manner, threatens the woman and her descendants (see Gen 3:15). Behind this wicked creature, whether serpent or dragon, hides the lion who prowls hungrily around God's chosen ones, to pounce on them in moments of weakness: "Like a roaring lion your adversary the devil prowls around, looking for someone to devour. Resist him, steadfast in your faith" (1 Pet 5:8–9). The enemy sets a trap for Adam and Eve, promising them illusions; now in the vision of the Book of Revelation, he sets a trap for the newborn Christians. Weak in faith, they need care and comfort as a newborn infant would. This text alludes to the crisis of the newborn community: not all Christians are up to facing persecution; not all resist the temptation to renounce their faith. We always live between certainty and doubt, strength and weakness, solidarity and egoism. The Apostle Paul knew it very well: "We are afflicted in every way, but not crushed; perplexed, but not driven to despair; persecuted, but not forsaken; struck down, but not destroyed" (2 Cor 4:8–9). The woman clothed with the sun is the Church, who continuously gives birth to new children through Baptism. The dragon with its mouth open wide symbolizes the persecution or tribulation that awaits those who have barely been born.

To make a covenant with Mary is not some devout game; it means taking our part in the struggle between the New Eve and the dragon! *To put ourselves on her side* means taking on a responsibility that must remain firm even when we are trapped by fear or danger: when our proclamation of the Gospel of the Crucified proves weak and our attempts fruitless, when the work to do is enormous, and when the evil that surrounds us threateningly seems invincible. This is why the great saints who were devoted to Mary never knew a moment's rest. But all their strength was already in their faith. They saw the victory when it was still impossible to perceive, and they knew that the Mother of the Lord had completely crushed the head of the serpent. For this reason they remained serene in the midst of storms. Ignoring fatigue, they reached the goal of their love.

To Bring Forth Life Like Mary: An Apostolic Mysticism

We give Christ to the world with our own weakness and in the context of an agonizing struggle, even if it often goes unnoticed. The only hope of succeeding is again found in the authentically evangelical form of our baptismal existence. The more we allow ourselves to be Christified by the Spirit, the more we will know how to generate Christ in others. The secret of this success is Trinitarian: if I let myself be taken up by Christ, I am necessarily projected outside of myself because Jesus is completely turned to the Father and to the brethren. I become an apostle because I make my own the apostolic soul of the Master. Real consecration to Mary requires that we become familiar with the two basic principles of what we could call apostolic mysticism: *intimacy* and *hiddenness*.

Let us immediately clear away some ambiguities. Intimacy must be properly understood. Elizabeth of the Trinity said that in Mary "everything took place on the inside." The sense here is that miracles of grace happened in her heart and transformed it. In Mary intimacy is the opposite of superficiality. Intimacy is the life of a person who founds his or her self-awareness on the sphere of the Spirit who cries in us "Abba! Father!" (Rom 8:15). Knowing oneself to be the son or daughter of this Father, one discerns and chooses according to the Gospel. Unfortunately, very few believers live this way. Most content themselves with some good thoughts, but they never get down to actually making daily decisions. And even when they do "good things," they do it in a way that happens to be seen by people (see Mt 6:1–18).

Without this intimacy with Christ, the apostolate is a caricature; it becomes a show. Mary gave her Son because she carried him in her womb. For her, the first apostle, giving Christ to the world was the irresistible result of a unique way of feeling herself involved in the very life of God, as happened to the prophet Amos:

> The lion has roared;
>> who will not fear?
> The Lord God has spoken;
>> who can but prophesy? (Am 3:8)

The visitation to Elizabeth undeniably reminds us: Some are *bearers of the Spirit* because *they are made spiritual.* We carry Christ because we have conceived him, thanks to the seed of the Word listened to and received. For this reason mysticism has to precede the apostolate and accompany it, inasmuch as locating ourselves in the life of the Spirit gives our actions the *flavor of God.* We are not far from the Master's teaching: "Abide in me as I abide in you. Just as the branch cannot bear fruit by itself unless it abides in the vine, neither can you unless you abide in me" (Jn 15:4). Blessed James Alberione had this in mind when, in an ingenious way, he defined the apostle as "the temple of the Holy Trinity who is in him and is supremely active."[13] Christ the Apostle *lives in me* when I do the apostolate, just as the baby *living in Mary* sanctified Elizabeth with his Spirit.

To live in intimacy has another aspect. Precisely because we experience the Spirit's action in us, we are led to highly esteem the means of grace in carrying out the apostolate. Certainly everyone needs to go about their mission and serve one's neighbor in a

---

13. Blessed James Alberione, *Ut perfectus sit homo Dei* (Milan, Cinisello Balsamo: Edizioni San Paolo, 1998), 519.

professional and organized way. Yet the person who lives with a "Mariform" Spirit in announcing the Gospel will give great importance to the sacraments, to intercessory prayer, to offering up sufferings for the good of one's neighbor (see Col 1:24). They will recall that Mary was the greatest and most perfect collaborator of the Redeemer simply by remaining in continual discernment and letting herself be formed by the words of her Son. This kind of "intimacy" means opening one's heart to the goodness and need for what were once called the passive virtues. These virtues entail an abandonment to Love that is and will always remain the most efficacious means for making the Lord known and loved. We are apostles because our names are written in heaven, not because the demons obey us (see Lk 10:20)!

Hiddenness is the second key term in apostolic mysticism (which becomes a Marian way of bringing the Lord). Venerable Jean-Claude Colin said this means being "unknown and almost hidden in this world."[14]

Let us seek to understand better this expression, which at first glance might seem outdated and forgotten. As we have already reflected, by her singular election and mission Mary is the key to the coming of Jesus and of the newborn Church. Her

---

14. The French priest Jean-Claude Colin (1790–1875) is the Founder of the Society of Mary or Marist Fathers. In the panorama of nineteenth-century spirituality, he is distinguished by his Marian emphasis in the priesthood: the priest lives in the world as the Mother of the Lord had her place in the heart of the family of Nazareth and in the Cenacle. Although his spirituality is very pertinent to our times, unfortunately it is almost completely unknown. See F. Gioannetti, *Jean Claude Colin fondatore dei P.P. Maristi. Una spirituality per il nostro tempo* (Rome: Curia Generalizia SM, 1985), 133–81.

contemplative faith can be found in the heart of the mystery of the incarnation and of Pentecost. She is Mother of the Head in the flesh, and Mother of the Body in the Spirit. This essential, efficacious presence has never been merely a show of charisms. Such is the paradox of the Virgin's service, which is necessary yet almost unknown, powerful yet very discreet. While around Jesus, everyone spoke to either acclaim or criticize him; the Virgin remained far from the clamor and empty words. Her presence in the newborn Church was so humble that people began to reflect seriously on it only after her death. We think of Mary as a key person in Christianity, but we forget that during her earthly life she remained the most unknown of all.[15]

The great Apostle Paul never speaks expressly of Mary. Her existence is surrounded by the absolutely normal and ordinary.

---

15. She is, of all the saints, the most perfectly poor and the most perfectly hidden, the only one who has absolutely nothing whatever that she attempts to possess as her own, that she can communicate most fully to the rest of us the grace of the infinitely selfless God. And we will most truly possess him when we have emptied ourselves and become poor and hidden as she is, resembling Him by resembling her.

And all our sanctity depends on her maternal love. The ones she desires to share the joy of her own poverty and simplicity, the ones whom she wills to be hidden as she is hidden, are the ones who share her closeness to God. . . . And the most precious of all the gifts of nature or grace is the desire to be hidden and to vanish from the sight of men and be accounted as nothing by the world and to disappear from one's own self-conscious consideration and vanish into nothingness in the immense poverty that is the adoration of God.

This absolute emptiness, this poverty, this obscurity holds within it the secret of all joy because it is full of God. To seek this emptiness is true devotion to the Mother of God. To find it is to find her. Thomas Merton, *New Seeds of Contemplation* (New York: New Directions Publishing, 2007), 173–74.

All Mary's glory on earth is enclosed in humility, the humility proper to great ones who are so free from expectations that they can allow themselves the glory of "being nothing." God exalts the little ones, hiding them from the world!

This marginal way of understanding oneself and of placing oneself in the heart of the Church *is the indispensable corollary that strengthens and protects intimacy with Christ. It saves the* Church from human expectations and from fragmentation. Perhaps this is the most important point for someone who, like Mary, wants to live by serving the community, to remain "unknown," avoiding the clamor, freeing oneself from the fear of not succeeding in a career. It means to love "hiddenness," like someone who does good with their left hand without the right hand knowing it (see Mt 6:3), saving oneself from the desire of being repaid and recognized. That is possible in dealings with others only if there is a way of relating to the Father in the secret of the heart, rejecting the admiration of others as Jesus commanded insistently (see Mt 6:4, 6, 18). Whoever lives in secret under the gaze of God is content to remain unknown and hidden in the heart of the Church. The two things go together and live of the same evangelical logic.

> *All Mary's glory*
> *on earth is enclosed*
> *in humility . . .*

Summary

Baptism marks the mystical birth of Jesus in us and unites us to the community of believers. The human nature and the divine nature of Jesus were united in Mary's womb without being confused. Similarly, in the baptismal font, grace invades our mortal flesh. Everything is made fruitful by the DNA of Christ, to be healed and reintegrated in the truth. The principle and foundation of our very spiritual breath, the journey of Christification we have been called to, can already be contemplated in the Christiform Mother. Her Immaculate Conception prefigures the Baptism of grace that washed us of our aversion to God. Her assumption and regal status in the Communion of Saints anticipates the entrance of our whole being into the Father's paradise, to take our place in the heavenly Church.

To give oneself to Mary is a response to the gift of the Crucified. To receive his Mother as our own involves the conscious choice of letting baptismal grace be completed so that Christ reaches full maturity in us. The free act by which we surrender to this transforming dynamic involves following the Master, renouncing oneself, and carrying one's cross. In a word, we have to choose for ourselves the humility and self-emptying of Jesus, his *kenosis*. "To take Mary into one's own house" and "to choose for oneself the abasement of the Son," the highest act of love possible to a creature, are virtually equivalent gestures. There is no Christianity without self-emptying, just as there is no Marian spirituality that rejects the mystery of the cross.

The baptismal gift begins the commitment to allow Christ to live in us, he who is the priest of humanity, the missionary of the Father. To give Jesus to others is the natural consequence of having met him. As Saint Vincent de Paul said, "It's not enough for me to love Christ if my neighbor does not love him."[16] Mary gave her Son, the only-begotten of the Father, after having conceived him. Mary, the model of the apostle, gives him to us, extending her arms. However Scripture does not permit us to be complacent. We announce grace to a world that often does not want it because it does not know it: "He came to what was his own, and his own people did not accept him" (Jn 1:11). Whoever dreams of success in the apostolate or counts numbers is a poor deluded person! Rarely do people applaud anyone who proclaims the truth taught by the Master. Cross and struggle against the apathy of indifference are the daily bread of the true apostle!

The apostolate of Mary possesses the unmistakable features of intimacy with Christ and of hiddenness. Because of this, in her there was not a simple "doing" but a particular *apostolic mysticism*. Her Christified being poured itself out in deeds that flowed naturally from the contemplative heart that was given to her. To paraphrase Saint Augustine, the Master was more intimate with her than she was with herself, for he breathed and acted in her even before being born. Her way of acting was already that of the

---

16. *Conferences of Vincent de Paul*, 581. Coste, XII, n. 207, On Charity, (May 30, 1659): 262. Found at http://vinformation.org/en/vincentian-spirituality/virtues-and-charism/quotations-2/#_edn87.

Son who humbled himself, taking the form of a slave. Thus the style of Mary's self-gift has to be hidden in the eyes of the world, far from every form of spiritual pride and vainglory.

Meditations

Of the essence of motherhood is the fact that it concerns the person. Motherhood always establishes a unique and unrepeatable relationship between two people: between mother and child and between child and mother. Even when the same woman is the mother of many children, her personal relationship with each one of them is of the very essence of motherhood. For each child is generated in a unique and unrepeatable way, and this is true both for the mother and for the child. Each child is surrounded in the same way by that maternal love on which are based the child's development and coming to maturity as a human being.

It can be said that motherhood "in the order of grace" preserves the analogy with what "in the order of nature" characterizes the union between mother and child. In the light of this fact it becomes easier to understand why in Christ's testament on Golgotha his Mother's new motherhood is expressed in the singular, in reference to one man: "Behold your son."

It can also be said that these same words fully show the reason for the Marian dimension of the life of Christ's disciples. This is true not only of John, who at that hour stood at the foot of the cross together with his Master's Mother, but it is also true of every disciple of Christ, of every Christian. The Redeemer entrusts his mother to the disciple, and at the same time he gives her to him as his mother. Mary's motherhood, which becomes man's inheritance, is a gift: a gift which Christ himself makes personally to every individual. The Redeemer

entrusts Mary to John because he entrusts John to Mary. At
the foot of the cross there begins that special entrusting of
humanity to the Mother of Christ, which in the history of the
Church has been practiced and expressed in different ways.
The same Apostle and Evangelist, after reporting the words
addressed by Jesus on the cross to his Mother and to himself,
adds: "And from that hour the disciple took her to his own
home" (Jn 19:27). This statement certainly means that the
role of son was attributed to the disciple and that he assumed
responsibility for the Mother of his beloved Master. And since
Mary was given as a mother to him personally, the statement
indicates, even though indirectly, everything expressed by the
intimate relationship of a child with its mother. And all of this
can be included in the word "entrusting." Such entrusting is
the response to a person's love, and in particular to the love of
a mother.

The Marian dimension of the life of a disciple of Christ is
expressed in a special way precisely through this filial entrusting to the Mother of Christ, which began with the testament
of the Redeemer on Golgotha. Entrusting himself to Mary in
a filial manner, the Christian, like the Apostle John, "wel-
comes" the Mother of Christ "into his own home"[17] and
brings her into everything that makes up his inner life, that is
to say into his human and Christian "I": he "took her to his

---

17. Clearly, in the Greek text the expression "*eis ta idia*" goes beyond the
mere acceptance of Mary by the disciple in the sense of material lodging and
hospitality in his house; it indicates rather a *communion of life* established
between the two as a result of the words of the dying Christ: cf. Saint Augustine,
In Ioan. Evang. Tract. 119, 3: *CCL* 36, 659: "He took her to himself, not into
his own property, for he possessed nothing of his own, but among his own
duties, which he attended to with dedication."

own home." Thus the Christian seeks to be taken into that "maternal charity" with which the Redeemer's Mother "cares for the brethren of her Son" (*LG*, 62), "in whose birth and development she cooperates" (*LG*, 63) in the measure of the gift proper to each one through the power of Christ's Spirit. Thus also is exercised that motherhood in the Spirit which became Mary's role at the foot of the cross and in the Upper Room.

Saint John Paul II, Encyclical Letter
Mother of the Redeemer, no. 45.

If Mary, who is the tree of life, is well cultivated in our soul by fidelity to the practices of this devotion, she will bear her fruit in her own time, and her fruit is none other than Jesus Christ. How many devout souls do I see who seek Jesus Christ, some by one way or by one practice, and others by other ways and other practices. After they have toiled much throughout the night, they say, "We have toiled all night, and have taken nothing"! We may say to them, "You have labored much, and gained little:" Jesus Christ is still seen only feebly in you. But by that immaculate way of Mary, and that divine practice which I am teaching, we toil during the day; we toil in a holy place; we toil but little. There is no darkness in Mary, because there is no sin, not even the slightest shadow. Mary is a holy place, and the holy of holies where saints are formed and molded.

Please notice that I say the saints are molded in Mary. There is a great difference between making a statue by blows of hammer and chisel, and making a statue by putting it into a mold. Sculptors labor much to make figures in the first way, but to make them in the second way, they work little, and do their work quickly.

Saint Augustine calls our Blessed Lady *forma Dei*—"the mold of God:"—"The mold fit to cast and mold gods." Whoever is cast in this mold is presently formed and molded in Jesus Christ, and Jesus Christ in him. At a slight expense and in a short time he will become like God, because he has been cast in the same mold that has formed a God-man.

By faithfully observing this practice, you will give Jesus more glory in a month than by any other practice, however difficult, in many years. I give the following reasons for saying this:

By doing your actions through our Blessed Lady, as this practice teaches you, you abandon your own intentions and operations, although good and known, to lose yourself, so to speak, in the intentions of the Blessed Virgin, although they are unknown. Thus you enter by participation into her sublime intentions. They are so pure that she gives more glory to God by the least of her actions—for example, in spinning wool or sewing—than Saint Lawrence by his cruel martyrdom on his gridiron, or even all the saints by all their heroic actions put together. That is why during her sojourn here below, she acquired such an unspeakable degree of graces and merits, that it would be easier to count the stars in heaven, the drops of water in the sea, or the grains of sand upon its shore, than her merits and graces. Thus she gave more glory to God than all the angels and saints have given him, or ever will give him. O Mary, a prodigy of God! You cannot help but work marvels of grace in souls that wish to lose themselves in you!

Saint Louis de Montfort,
True Devotion, nn. 218–219, 222.

The Six Apostolates of Mary

The first apostolate is a well-practiced interior life. The person who sanctifies himself is contributing to the whole Church, the mystical Body. For his part the holy person transfuses this body's circulation with a pure and immaculate blood. Because Mary is the holiest of creatures she contributed more than any others—apostles, martyrs, confessors, virgins—to edify and make the Church beautiful and dynamic. The interior life is the soul of every apostolate.

Second apostolate: prayer. Saint James says: "Pray for one another, so that you may be healed. The prayer of the righteous is powerful and effective" (Jas 5:16).

And Saint Paul: "First of all, then, I urge that supplications, prayers, intercessions, and thanksgivings be made for everyone. . . . This is right and is acceptable in the sight of God our Savior, who desires everyone to be saved and to come to the knowledge of the truth" (1 Tim 2:1, 3–4). And Mary prayed more than all, better than all, for the needs of all.

Third apostolate: good example. "Let your light shine before others, so that they may see your good works and give glory to your Father in heaven" (Mt 5:16). Someone wrote: "A person who is holy, perfect and virtuous does far greater good to souls than many other people who, though educated and active, have less spirit." Good example is silent preaching, which starts from life and goes on reforming life.

If words simply come out of your mouth they will only resound in a person's ears. Mary is our example in theological, cardinal, and religious virtues.

Fourth apostolate: suffering. Jesus Christ redeemed the world especially through his passion and death: "Through your holy cross and death you have redeemed the world." But there were two altars on Calvary: the cross of Jesus and the

Heart of Mary. A spear pierced the Heart of Jesus; a sword
pierced the soul of Mary. Father Faber uses this expression:
"Suffering is the greatest sacrament." In truth it is that which
gives value to the other sacraments. And all of us have so many
sufferings to offer to the Lord in a spirit of apostolate.

Fifth apostolate: the word. Mary did not preach, but she
certainly spoke with great charity and prudence at home and
outside of it. Of her we have seven words that are true apostolate, the Magnificat being a special example. The Fathers tell us
that it was Mary who revealed to Saint Luke the Gospel's
infancy narratives. Even today every word of hers is light for
contemplative souls.

Sixth apostolate: action. Mary's life before the Incarnation and during the thirty-three years passed with Jesus is an
ongoing series of acts and deeds aimed at accomplishing her
mission, her great apostolate. In the days following Jesus'
Ascension, in the Cenacle, and during the period of early
opposition and uncertainty when the Church was taking its
first steps, it was Mary who consoled, comforted, and encour-
aged the Apostles. No Catholic woman will accomplish
among women such activity, zeal, and instruction as did Mary
among the women and young pious disciples of her Divine
Son—right up to the end of her earthly mission.

Blessed James Alberione[18]

---

18. James Alberione, *Ut perfectus sit homo Dei,* op. cit., 516–18.

Conclusion

— • • • —

"Maybe we believe in the love of God and in the love of the Virgin, but not deep down. Maybe we even doubt that this love is effective enough to overcome all difficulties. That is why even if we live our abandonment, it is not perfectly peaceful. Yet God has given us infinitely more than we could have hoped. He has given us a Mother."[1]

With these words of Father Divo Barsotti, I find the help I need to conclude this brief work on the presence of *Jesus living in Mary* in our life as baptized persons. I would like to focus my thoughts on two points: disappointment and strength. I will begin with the first.

As Barsotti wrote, if we fail to entrust ourselves deep down, perhaps it is because we haven't touched the depths of

---

1. Divo Barsotti, *Maria nel mistero del Cristo. Meditazione* (Milan, Cinisello Balsamo: Edizioni San Paolo, 2009), 114.

disappointment. To entrust ourselves to God we must mistrust ourselves. There is no other road to the land of grace. This is the pathway that the sovereign Spirit made Peter walk. Thanks to the "empty nets," he was disappointed in his life as a fisherman, but then he had a memorable experience of the Master in his boat (see Lk 5:1–11). Then Peter was disappointed due to his mistaken ideas about Christ's mission (for which the Lord reproved him with unusual severity; see Mt 16:21–23). In the end, after his betrayal, Peter mistrusted his own self-confidence: "Lord, you know everything; you know that I love you" (Jn 21:17). Peter's experience touches all of the fundamental points of the self-emptying that makes us ready to re-clothe ourselves with Christ: from renouncing a little dream of a secure life, but one without horizons, to discovering that our fear is stronger than fidelity. And that's good. Overcoming illusions gives a gift—to those who accept it in truth—of authentic liberty, which rests entirely in choosing to depend on the one who loves you. The rest is a distortion.

Entrusting oneself to Mary places us within this existential framework. But it is not the *last resort*, in the sense that we place ourselves in her hands because we don't know what saint to turn to. To have Mary enter one's interior house is rather the *first choice*. The Spirit begins to whisper in us when we finally decide that mistrust of our ego is not the point where we end, but where we begin. It's not that we entrust ourselves to Mary because "there's nothing left to do," but precisely because there's so much to do. Only those who have discovered, with simplicity, that they are lacking before God know this, just as the tax collector in the

Temple (see Lk 18:13). Mary is the *refuge of sinners*, of those who remain such. The insensitive just ones and perhaps even some professional theologians are ignorant of this. Even for them grace always precedes . . . but only in theory! When we put ourselves in Mary's hands, as did the infant Jesus, the Innocent One, then everything really begins. Everything is newly conceived and we are open to true life, not to fantasies or fears. The old things disappear to make room for the new (2 Cor 5:17).

The second reflection crystallizes around the question of *strength*, the gift of the Spirit so necessary above all to serve and love the Church. Who is strong when faced with life? Who is bold enough to hold it? Who remains standing in the midst of scandals? Maybe strength is only a question of good luck, in the sense that we are quick to think ourselves strong when life hasn't beaten us up very much. As the saying goes, "Tribulations make one strong," but I would add, "especially those who don't experience them." Being strong with three square meals a day is not the same as being strong while fasting.

Some might suspect that devotion to Mary is only for the weak. We imagine this devotion as a kind of reassuring maternal warmth that risks leaving us in a state of infantile irresponsibility. In reality, the evangelical figure of the Virgin Mary has much strength, much more than other figures of the sacred texts. Mary has a divine strength precisely because her strength comes from God, who aids the weak while leaving them in their vulnerability (see 2 Cor 12:9). Let us ask our Mother for the strength that helped Joseph to take her as his bride. We can't do this alone. The Calvaries we must climb would be too steep, the difficult parts distant from community support . . . and we very uncertain. And then the Kingdom is a matter of the strong because only the violent can take hold of it (see Mt 11:12).

If that were not enough, we should also consider the strength needed to remain Christian in the midst of a world that is often hostile to Jesus' message. There is a subtle and prevailing conviction that the Gospel obstructs the achievement of civil rights. Christianity and liberty have been maliciously set at odds, as if they were irreconcilable. It is often insinuated that faith and personal happiness are incompatible. Ignorance reigns in this area. May Mary, the Queen of powerful intercession, rule within us, hesitant apostles, as she did in the Cenacle with those poor, failed disciples after the resurrection of her Son!

Let us begin to mistrust our ego and put complete confidence in Christ. These two focal points of the spiritual journey bring together in a proper perspective all the scattered pieces of existence, teaching us the profound sense of living in Christ and entrusting ourselves to Mary, the *form*. By ridding ourselves of the deceit of our *ego* and its sadness, I can run decisively toward the Eternal King and his Mother. One day, having arrived before his majesty, I will find myself awaited from eternity. Approaching the light, the heavenly court of the saints will encourage me to take the place prepared for me in the banquet of the Kingdom. Then I will taste the joy of being able to say, like the Samaritan woman, that I have met him "who told me everything I have ever done!" (Jn 4:29), and who, passing through the valley of tears changed it into a font of life-giving water (see Ps 84:7).

Five Characteristics of Christian Life in Mary

As we grow in our devotion to Mary, we can better reflect her virtues. The points below can serve as a sort of examination in this regard.

Purity of Heart

- To be so fascinated by the glory of God that one can let go of a self-will filled with outlandish dreams of greatness, so that only God's desire might be accomplished.

- To reject the duplicity and malice that leads us to become good servants in the Father's house while secretly hoping to take over one day.

- To understand profoundly that carving a place for oneself is the last resort of those who fail, and that true wisdom is to remain in one's own small place, making it great by faithfulness and unselfish acts.

- To desire to be so hidden that only God shines across the horizon of existence.

Gratitude

- To be so little as to know how to be thankful, learning to desire only what one already possesses.

- To accept all that has happened to us as coming from the hands of God, thanking him for his untiring fidelity that never ceases to be concerned about us.

- To stop spinning my wheels in the ditch of sadness and anger.

- To thank the Father for what he has given us, and to be grateful even for all that has been taken from us, making us freer.

Humility

- To live without fear in the paradox of what we are—persons "full of grace" but "who count for nothing," bearers of a treasure in earthen vessels.

- To celebrate our failures as if they were triumphs, seeing, as Mary did, from Calvary's heights the faint but certain light of Easter.

- To know how to look at the past with its blessings, and not to accuse others of faults for which we are responsible.

- To desire that others might know our sins, realizing that only when we are stripped even of honor can we say that we have touched, like Mary, the humble flesh of the Son of God.

Docility

- To be so humble that we can easily accept the dismissal of our good, idealistic projects, and let go of our demand that the Lord must make us saints in the way we want.

- Once we have died to ourselves, to cling wholeheartedly to the mysteries of Jesus' life, to relive them mystically, from the manger to the empty tomb.

- To give him the gift of our existence so that he might relive in us his own gift unto the end.

- To be wise enough to give up wanting to understand everything.

- To become so evangelically shrewd that we can be silent and ponder in our hearts even the most scandalous and unsavory things. To find God in everything.

Paternity/Maternity

- To shake off fears born of illusions and dreams that grow from the evil plant of pride.

- To go out from our own little world and enter that of Jesus, who desires to live within us. To allow him to sanctify people's expectations, as his Mother did with Elizabeth.

* To love the good of others so much that we spend everything, even to the point of having nothing left to offer and going broke, giving all that we are.

* To disappear completely, like Saint Joseph, the spouse of Mary, the foster-father of our one and glorious Lord.

Prayers of Blessed James Alberione

As a conclusion, I would like to quote some prayers of Blessed Alberione that fully express the content of the preceding pages. You will note that some of the expressions seem dated . . . but they are far from insignificant. At times it's good to make an effort to understand some terms that seem strange to us, in order to savor the fullness of their theological and spiritual meaning. For this reason, I did not consider it necessary to re-write any of the prayers.

Thanksgiving after Communion

Jesus my Life, my joy, and source of all good, I love you. Above all, I ask of you that I may love you more and more and all those redeemed by your blood.

You are the vine and I am the branch: I want to remain united to you always so as to bear much fruit.

You are the source: pour out an ever greater abundance of grace to sanctify my soul.

You are my head, I your member: communicate to me your Holy Spirit with all his gifts.

May your Kingdom come through Mary. May everyone enter your school, O Divine Master, our Way, Truth, and Life.

Console and save those dear to me. Free the souls in purgatory. Multiply and sanctify those called to the apostolate.

For Ministers of the Word

O Mary, you who gave birth to the Word made flesh, be present among us. Assist, inspire, and comfort the ministers of the word.

O Mary, you who are Queen of the Apostles, intervene with your protection that the light of the Gospel may reach all peoples.

O Mary, Mother of Jesus Way, Truth, and Life, intercede for us, that heaven may be filled with souls who sing the hymn of glory to the most Holy Trinity.

To Mary Queen of Apostles

Immaculate Mary, co-redemptrix of the human race, look upon humanity redeemed by the blood of your divine Son, yet still immersed in the darkness of error and confusion.

The harvest is always great, but the laborers are still very few. Have pity, O Mary, upon your children whom the dying Jesus entrusted to you from the cross. Increase religious and priestly vocations; give us new apostles full of wisdom and fervor. Sustain with your maternal care those who consecrate their lives to the good of their neighbor. Recall your care for Jesus and the Apostle John; remember your consoling presence on the day of Pentecost. You were the counselor of the first apostles and of the Apostles of all times. By your omnipotent intercession, obtain a new Pentecost for all those called to the apostolate, that it may sanctify them and inflame them with holy zeal for the glory of God and the salvation of humanity.

Guide them in all their efforts; aid them with your graces; sustain them in moments of discouragement; crown their zeal with great success.

Grant our prayer, O Mary, so that everyone may accept the Divine Master, Way and Truth and Life, and become docile members of the Catholic Church. May the whole world resound with your praises and honor you as Mother, Teacher, and Queen. Thus may we all attain eternal happiness in heaven. Amen.

To Mary Refuge of Sinners

Our tender Mother Mary, gate of heaven, source of peace and happiness, help of Christians, trust of the dying, and hope even of the desperate, I recall the blessed moment for you in which you left the earth to fly to the blessed embrace of Jesus. It was the omnipotent favor of God that assumed you into heaven, beautiful and immortal. I see you exalted above the angels and saints, confessors and virgins, apostles and martyrs, prophets and patriarchs, and even I, from the midst of my sins, dare to add the voice of an unworthy but repentant sinner to praise and bless you. O Mary, convert me once and for always. Give me a repentant life, that I may have a holy death and one day join my voice to that of the saints to praise you in heaven. I consecrate myself to you and through you to Jesus. With full awareness and here in the presence of all the heavenly court, I renew the promises made in holy Baptism. I renew the resolution, which I place in your heart, to fight my self-love and to combat unceasingly against my principal defect, which so often has cast me into sin. O Mary, gain for yourself the greatest glory: change a great sinner into a great saint, O refuge of sinners, O morning star, O comforter of the afflicted.

Queen of Apostles, pray for us.

Consecration to the Queen of Apostles

Receive me, Mary, Mother, Teacher, and Queen, among those whom you love, nourish, sanctify and guide, in the school of Jesus Christ, the Divine Master.

You identify in God's mind those whom he calls, and for them you have special prayers, grace, light, and consolations.

My Master, Jesus Christ, entrusted himself wholly to you, from the incarnation to the ascension.

For me this is doctrine, example, and an ineffable gift. I too place myself entirely into your hands.

Obtain for me the grace to know, imitate, and love ever more the Divine Master, Way and Truth and Life.

Present me to Jesus, for I am an unworthy sinner, and I have no other recommendation to be admitted to his school than your recommendation.

Enlighten my mind, fortify my will, sanctify my heart, during this year of my spiritual work, so that I may profit from this great mercy, and may say at the end: "I live now not I, but Christ lives in me."

Saint Paul the Apostle, my father and most faithful disciple of Jesus, strengthen me. I want to do my utmost, my very utmost, so that Jesus Christ may be formed in me. Amen.

BOOKS & MEDIA

The Daughters of St. Paul operate book and media centers at the following addresses. Visit, call, or write the one nearest you today, or find us at www.paulinestore.org.

CALIFORNIA

3908 Sepulveda Blvd, Culver City, CA 90230	310-397-8676
3250 Middlefield Road, Menlo Park, CA 94025	650-369-4230

FLORIDA

145 S.W. 107th Avenue, Miami, FL 33174	305-559-6715

HAWAII

1143 Bishop Street, Honolulu, HI 96813	808-521-2731

ILLINOIS

172 North Michigan Avenue, Chicago, IL 60601	312-346-4228

LOUISIANA

4403 Veterans Memorial Blvd, Metairie, LA 70006	504-887-7631

MASSACHUSETTS

885 Providence Hwy, Dedham, MA 02026	781-326-5385

MISSOURI

9804 Watson Road, St. Louis, MO 63126	314-965-3512

NEW YORK

115 E. 29th Street, New York City, NY 10016	212-754-1110

SOUTH CAROLINA

243 King Street, Charleston, SC 29401	843-577-0175

TEXAS

No book center; for parish exhibits or outreach evangelization, contact: 210-569-0500, or SanAntonio@paulinemedia.com, or P.O. Box 761416, San Antonio, TX 78245

VIRGINIA

1025 King Street, Alexandria, VA 22314	703-549-3806

CANADA

3022 Dufferin Street, Toronto, ON M6B 3T5	416-781-9131

¡También somos su fuente para libros,
videos y música en español!